THE BUSINESS CASE FOR E-LEARNING

Tom Kelly, Nader Nanjiani

Cisco Press

800 East 96th Street
Indianapolis, Indiana 46240 USA

The Business Case for E-Learning

Tom Kelly, Nader Nanjiani

Copyright© 2005 Cisco Systems, Inc.

Published by:
Cisco Press
800 East 96th Street
Indianapolis, IN 46240 USA

All rights reserved. No part of this book may be reproduced or transmitted in any form or by any means, electronic or mechanical, including photocopying, recording, or by any information storage and retrieval system, without written permission from the publisher, except for the inclusion of brief quotations in a review.

Printed in the United States of America 1 2 3 4 5 6 7 8 9 0
First Printing October 2004
Library of Congress Cataloging-in-Publication Number: 2003100133
ISBN: 1-58720-086-4

Warning and Disclaimer

This book is designed to provide information about e-learning. Every effort has been made to make this book as complete and as accurate as possible, but no warranty or fitness is implied.

The information is provided on an "as is" basis. The authors, Cisco Press, and Cisco Systems, Inc. shall have neither liability nor responsibility to any person or entity with respect to any loss or damages arising from the information contained in this book or from the use of the discs or programs that may accompany it.

The opinions expressed in this book belong to the author and are not necessarily those of Cisco Systems, Inc.

Feedback Information

At Cisco Press, our goal is to create in-depth technology management books of the highest quality and value. Each book is crafted with care and precision, undergoing rigorous development that involves the unique expertise of members from the professional technical community.

Readers' feedback is a natural continuation of this process. If you have any comments regarding how we could improve the quality of this book, or otherwise alter it to better suit your needs, you can contact us through email at feedback@ciscopress.com. Please make sure to include the book title and ISBN in your message.

We greatly appreciate your assistance.

Trademark Acknowledgments

All terms mentioned in this book that are known to be trademarks or service marks have been appropriately capitalized. Cisco Press or Cisco Systems, Inc. cannot attest to the accuracy of this information. Use of a term in this book should not be regarded as affecting the validity of any trademark or service mark.

Corporate and Government Sales

Cisco Press offers excellent discounts on this book when ordered in quantity for bulk purchases or special sales.

For more information please contact: U.S. Corporate and Government Sales 1-800-382-3419 corpsales@pearsontechgroup.com

For sales outside the U.S. please contact: International Sales international@pearsoned.com

Publisher	John Wait
Editor-in-Chief	John Kane
Cisco Representative	Anthony Wolfenden
Cisco Press Program Manager	Nannette M. Noble
Production Manager	Patrick Kanouse
Development Editor	Ginny Bess
Senior Project Editor	San Dee Phillips
Copy Editor	Keith Cline
Technical Editors	Richard Hezel, Wayne Hodgins, Ron Kovac
Editorial Assistant	Tammi Barnett
Book and Cover Designer	Louisa Adair
Compositor	Mark Shirar
Indexer	Tim Wright

CISCO SYSTEMS

Corporate Headquarters
Cisco Systems, Inc.
170 West Tasman Drive
San Jose, CA 95134-1706
USA
www.cisco.com
Tel: 408 526-4000
   800 553-NETS (6387)
Fax: 408 526-4100

European Headquarters
Cisco Systems International BV
Haarlerbergpark
Haarlerbergweg 13-19
1101 CH Amsterdam
The Netherlands
www-europe.cisco.com
Tel: 31 0 20 357 1000
Fax: 31 0 20 357 1100

Americas Headquarters
Cisco Systems, Inc.
170 West Tasman Drive
San Jose, CA 95134-1706
USA
www.cisco.com
Tel: 408 526-7660
Fax: 408 527-0883

Asia Pacific Headquarters
Cisco Systems, Inc.
Capital Tower
168 Robinson Road
#22-01 to #29-01
Singapore 068912
www.cisco.com
Tel: +65 6317 7777
Fax: +65 6317 7799

Cisco Systems has more than 200 offices in the following countries and regions. Addresses, phone numbers, and fax numbers are listed on the Cisco.com Web site at www.cisco.com/go/offices.

Argentina • Australia • Austria • Belgium • Brazil • Bulgaria • Canada • Chile • China PRC • Colombia • Costa Rica • Croatia • Czech Republic • Denmark • Dubai, UAE • Finland • France • Germany • Greece • Hong Kong SAR • Hungary • India • Indonesia • Ireland • Israel • Italy • Japan • Korea • Luxembourg • Malaysia • Mexico • The Netherlands • New Zealand • Norway • Peru • Philippines • Poland • Portugal • Puerto Rico • Romania • Russia • Saudi Arabia • Scotland • Singapore • Slovakia • Slovenia • South Africa • Spain • Sweden • Switzerland • Taiwan • Thailand • Turkey • Ukraine • United Kingdom • United States • Venezuela • Vietnam • Zimbabwe

Copyright © 2003 Cisco Systems, Inc. All rights reserved. CCIP, CCSP, the Cisco Arrow logo, the Cisco *Powered* Network mark, the Cisco Systems Verified logo, Cisco Unity, Follow Me Browsing, FormShare, iQ Net Readiness Scorecard, Networking Academy, and ScriptShare are trademarks of Cisco Systems, Inc.; Changing the Way We Work, Live, Play, and Learn, The Fastest Way to Increase Your Internet Quotient, and iQuick Study are service marks of Cisco Systems, Inc.; and Aironet, ASIST, BPX, Catalyst, CCDA, CCDP, CCIE, CCNA, CCNP, Cisco, the Cisco Certified Internetwork Expert logo, Cisco IOS, the Cisco IOS logo, Cisco Press, Cisco Systems, Cisco Systems Capital, the Cisco Systems logo, Empowering the Internet Generation, Enterprise/Solver, EtherChannel, EtherSwitch, Fast Step, GigaStack, Internet Quotient, IOS, IP/TV, iQ Expertise, the iQ logo, LightStream, MGX, MICA, the Networkers logo, Network Registrar, *Packet*, PIX, Post-Routing, Pre-Routing, RateMUX, Registrar, SlideCast, SMARTnet, StrataView Plus, Stratm, SwitchProbe, TeleRouter, TransPath, and VCO are registered trademarks of Cisco Systems, Inc. and/or its affiliates in the U.S. and certain other countries.

All other trademarks mentioned in this document or Web site are the property of their respective owners. The use of the word partner does not imply a partnership relationship between Cisco and any other company. (0303R)

Printed in the USA

About the Authors

Tom Kelly is vice president at Internet Learning Solutions at Cisco Systems, Inc., which is responsible for deploying training to the direct sales force, channel partners, and customers on Cisco products, systems, and solutions. In addition, his team manages the Cisco Career Certification Program for networking professionals. He is also responsible for driving and evangelizing Cisco best practices associated with e-learning technologies and the business impacts that result.

Joining Cisco in 1997, Tom launched the Cisco Career Certification Program in April 1998, resulting in the certification of more than 670,000 Associate, Professional, and Expert level network engineers as of September 2004. In 1999, he established the Field E-Learning Connection, a specialized website that offered 90 percent of the training needed by the Cisco Sales Force and has over 20,000 employee subscribers, and the Partner E-Learning Connection for Cisco Reseller partners with over 160,000 unique users. Other initiatives include the creation of the Cisco Media Network (live video to every desktop), cosponsoring the Cisco global video-on-demand implementation, the launch and delivery of Cisco Business Video Solution, the creation of learning games, and a focus on enabling remote collaboration systems.

Prior to joining Cisco, Tom was vice president of the Education Products Division at Oracle Corporation; prior to that, he had similar leadership and management roles at Sun Microsystems, NeXT Corporation, and Control Data Corporation over his 24 years in the education and training industry.

Kelly earned B.S. and M.B.A. degrees from Saint Cloud State University in St. Cloud, Minnesota.

Tom lives with his wife, Suzanne, and their new baby in Palo Alto, California.

Nader Abbas Nanjiani is the marketing programs manager of the Internet Learning Solutions Group, Cisco Systems, Inc. He has worked in the area of e-learning for more than a decade. Nader currently manages the Career Certifications program for Cisco Systems. He has worked at Cisco for four years.

While at Cisco, Nader developed and launched Cisco Certifications Community—a knowledge sharing portal with lifelong learning tools for certified individuals. More than 50,000 certified individuals signed up to the site in its first year. The Community offers tools such as a monthly "Certifications Connect" Web TV show, online learning games, discussion forums, and recertification alerts for its members.

Before joining Cisco, Nader worked for NEC America where he was responsible for increasing the visibility and adoption of NEC's voice, video, and data products in the education market. While working for Hezel Associates prior to NEC, Nader managed consulting projects on e-learning for corporate, government, and educational clients such as Tulane University, the World Bank, University of Texas System, Houghton-Mifflin, and the U.S. Department of Education.

Nader has published numerous articles on e-learning and certifications. He's a frequent speaker on e-learning for Cisco at technology conferences and was also featured on CNBC-Asia in 2003.

Nader received an M.S. degree in Television/Radio from Syracuse University and an M.B.A. degree from Karachi University, Karachi, Pakistan.

Nader lives with his wife and two sons outside of Dallas, Texas. Nader is an avid long-distance runner—he completed three marathons in the course of co-authoring this book!

About the Technical Reviewers

Dr. Richard T. Hezel is president and founder of Hezel Associates, LLC. He has directed market analyses, evaluations, needs assessments, and strategic planning for many national and international clients, including the World Health Organization, Habitat for Humanity, PBS, West Virginia Department of Education, JASON Foundation, and U.S. Department of Education. In addition, Richard has conducted strategic services and consulting within many states and organizations, at the K-12, higher education, and corporate levels of learning.

Richard gained recognition as a national expert for his writing and speaking on distance learning policy, management, and development in all fifty states. His company has published *Educational Telecommunications and Distance Learning: The State-By-State Analysis*. He is the author of numerous papers and reports on telecommunications research, management, and policy and has been a speaker at conferences and industry meetings throughout the United States, Canada, Philippines, Germany, and United Kingdom. He is a member of the National University Telecommunications Network and United States Distance Learning Association Board of Directors. His company is fully engaged in the e-learning community as a corporate member of WCET, UCEA, AECT, and ASTD.

Prior to establishing Hezel Associates, Richard was an associate professor of telecommunications and director of the graduate program in Public Communications Studies at the S.I. Newhouse School of Public Communications at Syracuse University. He served as an assistant professor at the University of Houston's School of Communications. He began his career in public broadcasting as television producer/director.

A native of Buffalo, NY, Richard earned a doctoral degree in mass communication from Indiana University. He received a master's degree in television and radio from Syracuse University and a bachelor's degree in history from Fordham University.

Wayne Hodgins is recognized around the world as a strategic futurist and one of the leading experts on human performance improvement, knowledge management, and learning and training technology. With more than 30-years of experience in business and education, Wayne has developed thought-provoking and visionary perspectives on how learning, technology, and standards can revolutionize work-force productivity.

As a strategic futurist for Autodesk, Inc., the world's leading digital design company, Wayne has worked with numerous Fortune 500 companies, government agencies, and high-tech companies to develop learning, training, and technology strategies. He is at the forefront of learning technology standards, serving as chairman of the IEEE Learning Technology Standards Committee. IEEE recognized Wayne in 2004 with its prestigious *Hans Karlsson Award for Leadership and Achievement through Collaboration* for his work in defining the Learning Object Metadata Standard, the world's first accredited standard for learning and technology. Wayne also serves as a strategic advisor to groups such as the U.S. Department of Defense, CEN/ISSS European Standards Body, PROMETEUS education and training consortium for Europe, ISO JTC1/SC36, and Advanced Learning Infrastructure Consortium in Japan.

Wayne has been profiled and interviewed by business press including Forbes, Fortune, Industry Week, CNN, C-NET, and e-CFO. *Training Magazine* named Wayne one its top 10 "New Breed of Visionaries for the 21st Century," and *e-Learning Magazine* recognized Wayne as a corporate learning leader by naming him one of the "Top 10 CLOs."

Dr. Ron Kovac is a full professor at the Center for Information and Communication Sciences at Ball State University in Indiana. The Center prepares graduate students in the field of telecommunications. Previously, he was the telecommunication manager for the State of New York and a CIO for a large east coast computing center. Ron's previous studies included electrical engineering, photography, and education. He has numerous publications (2 books and over 50 articles) and has completed numerous international consulting projects in both the education and telecommunications field. Additionally, he speaks worldwide on issues related to telecommunications and holds numerous certifications including the CCNA, CCAI, and the almost complete CCNP.

Dedications

Tom Kelly's dedication
To my wife, Suzanne, who understands, supports, and shares the passions that fuel a focus on learning and efforts to improve how we all teach and learn.

Nader Nanjiani's dedication
To my parents, Shehnaz and Ashfaq Nanjiani, for always knowing that learning and education offer some of the best returns on investment in life.

Acknowledgments

Everything we do at Cisco is a team effort. That's not because we don't believe in individual accountability, but because it doesn't make sense to do it by yourself when you have access to a pool of talented professionals. We don't always see things the same way, but the end product is made better by overcoming challenges.

Writing this book was also a team effort. A few of us might have owned it, but a number of individuals offered support. Not only did we receive immense assistance within Cisco, but also from outside. Our partners, colleagues, associates, and friends from outside of Cisco offered their best advice in helping with our efforts.

Thanks for making it happen

Piper Gianola of Cisco Systems is easily the person without whom the book would not have been possible. She saw the opportunity for a book in this area and got us working together. John Kane, our publisher from Cisco Press, is perhaps one of the most, if not the most, supportive, encouraging, and collaborative partners we've worked with in a long time. And, of course, thanks to Don Field, whose slide deck and comments at a conference got the discussion rolling in the first place.

Thanks for contributing, Cisco team

Special thanks to Chuck Battipede, Diane Bauer, Lisa Baumert, Rick Crowley, Meg Epstein, Don Hazel, Brendon Hynes, Karen Janowski, Susan Jeannero, Mike Mitchell, Bill Parkhurst, Yolanda Salas, and Matt Tabor for their contributions toward the discussion and case studies in the book. Thanks Sonia Chavez, JoAnn Wilson, and Anthony Wolfenden for keeping the project on track. We appreciate the help of Delcina Betts, Matt O'Donohue, Corrin Hastings, Peg Maddocks, Jay Meissner, Mike Metz, and Lyle Speirs who offered encouragement and review of early drafts.

Thanks for keeping us honest

Thanks to Dr. Richard Hezel, Wayne Hodgins, and Ron Kovac for their critical review and input. Lori Bistis was great with her friendly feedback. Thanks to Ginny Bess for her attention to detail and keen follow-up and to San Dee Phillips for her production efforts. Tim Sosbe and Gary Byrd were great at making sure that we stay focused on the small matter of audience interest throughout the writing process.

Thanks for letting us

With full-time jobs, travel, growing families, and chores around the house, the added task of writing a book is probably about the last thing a family needs to pencil in when struggling to spend more time together! As we poured over the chapters on vacation days and weekends, we couldn't have done it without the support and understanding of our respective spouses who encouraged us to take the time to say what we felt needed to be said.

Contents at a Glance

       Introduction xix
       Prologue xvii

Part I   Understanding the Business Impact of E-Learning

Chapter 1   Vaulted: From the Classroom to the Boardroom   1

Chapter 2   Internet Learning—A Productivity Tool   17

Chapter 3   E-Learning Under the Microscope   33

Part II   Business Success with E-Learning

Chapter 4   BearingPoint Makes a Grand Slam with Internet Learning: A Case Study   57

Chapter 5   Learner Driven at the University of Toyota: Pioneers of Just-in-Time Advocate "Hands-On" Skills   69

Chapter 6   E-Learning Goes Global: Networking Academy Transforms Lives   77

Chapter 7   Targeted Learning: Are You *Indeed* Ready?   87

Chapter 8   Productivity in the Extended Enterprise: Internet Learning Offers a Competitive Edge with Channel Partners   95

Chapter 9   Picking a Networking Dream Team   109

Chapter 10   Certifications as a Branding Tool: Sponsoring a Certification Program   117

Part III   Deploying Your E-Learning Efforts: Best Practices

Chapter 11   The Building Blocks   131

Chapter 12   Organizing an Internet Learning Initiative   141

Chapter 13   Building an Internet Learning Solution   157

Chapter 14   Practitioners' Views on the Business Advantages of E-Learning   173

Epilogue   183

Index   185

Contents

        Introduction xix

        Prologue   xvii

Part I   Understanding the Business Impact of E-Learning

Chapter 1   Vaulted: From the Classroom to the Boardroom   1
               A Once-in-a-Hundred-Year Flood: After the Bubble   2
               The Three Waves of E-Learning at Cisco   3
                   The Productivity Imperative   6
                       The Net Impact of Productivity   6
                       Employee Productivity Through Internet Learning   8
                   A C-Level Perspective: Banking on the Knowledge Worker   10
                   The Promise of E-Learning: Learning in Lean Times   11
               Internet Learning: Options and Alternatives   12
               End Notes   16

Chapter 2   Internet Learning—A Productivity Tool   17
               Charting a Course   18
               Synergy   19
               A Matter of Semantics   20
               The Scope of Productivity Improvements   21
                   The Advantages from an Employer Perspective   22
                   The Advantages from an Employee Perspective   24
               No Technology Religion   26
               A Premium on Skills   28
               Learner Driven More Than Learner Centric   29
               Target Audiences   30
               End Notes   31

Chapter 3   E-Learning Under the Microscope   33
               Benefits of Formulating a Business Case   34
               E-Communication   36
                   Beyond Awareness: Retention and Motivation   37
                   Video over IP: An E-Communication Breakthrough   39
               E-Training   41
               E-Assessment   48

Determining a Value on Investment for E-Learning 51
  Arriving at the Numbers 52
  Principles Behind the Numbers 53
Conclusion 55
Endnotes 55

Part II Business Success with E-Learning

Chapter 4 BearingPointMakes a Grand Slam with Internet Learning: A Case Study 57
Case Summary 58
Introduction 59
The Point of Inflexion 59
Building on Success 61
Nimble and Productive 62
What's in Store? 63
Look Out, Land Mines Ahead 64
Ways of Winning in the Enterprise 65
Recommendations on Leading E-Learning 66
Conclusion 67

Chapter 5 Learner Driven at the University of Toyota: Pioneers of Just-in-Time Advocate "Hands-On" Skills 69
Case Summary 70
Background 70
Just-in-Time Learning: A Business Function at Toyota 71
Cost-Effective Business Model 72
Even "Know-It-Alls" Can't Escape 72
Deploying a Productivity Cycle at Toyota 73
Conclusion 76

Chapter 6 E-Learning Goes Global: Networking Academy Transforms Lives 77
Case Summary 78
Background 78
How the Program Works 80
  Industry-Responsive Curriculum 80
  Train-the-Trainer Model 80
  Blended Learning with E-Assessment 81
  Underserved Segment 82

	Impact of the Program 82
	Benefits to Cisco 83
	Changing Lives One Life at a Time 84
	Conclusion 86
Chapter 7	Targeted Learning: Are You *Indeed* Ready? 87
	Case Summary 88
	Rationale Behind Targeted Learning 88
	From "Best Trained" to "Most Competent" 89
	The Development Cycle: A Three-Step Process 90
	Learning Portals for Productivity: Facilitating the Manager 92
	Conclusion 94
Chapter 8	Productivity in the Extended Enterprise: Internet Learning Offers a Competitive Edge with Channel Partners 95
	Case Summary 96
	The Value Proposition 97
	A Program That Rewards Learning 97
	The Learning Challenge 98
	PEC: A Viable Learning Solution 98
	Feedback About PEC 101
	Business Benefits of PEC 103
	Recommendations for Building an Extended Enterprise 105
	Conclusion 107
Chapter 9	Picking a Networking Dream Team 109
	Integration Challenge at Equant 112
	Merger Relied on Talent 112
	Certified Talent Delivers Results 113
	Benefits to Equant 114
	Conclusion 114
	Endnotes 115
Chapter 10	Certifications as a Branding Tool: Sponsoring a Certification Program 117
	Certifying Partners or Resellers at Cisco 119

Creating a Certification Program   122
Developing a Certification Program   123
Conclusion   130
Endnote   130

Part III   Deploying Your E-Learning Efforts: Best Practices

Chapter 11   The Building Blocks   131
Begin with Knowledge-Sharing Tools:
   E-Communications   132
Functional Integration   133
Cross-Functional Management   133
Technical Tools and Capabilities   134
Content Life Cycle Management   134
Distributed Authoring   135
Skills Gap Analysis   135
Learner Buy-In   136
Locus of Control   137
Conclusion   140

Chapter 12   Organizing an Internet Learning Initiative   141
Prepare a Case for Internet Learning in Your
   Organization   143
Senior Management Sponsorship   148
Assess Build Versus Buy Options   150
Implement the Pilot   151
Measure and Report Tangible Results   152
Prepare a Proposal for Expanding the Pilot   152
Ongoing Governance   152
Implement for Results   154
   Build to Scale   154
   Aim to Integrate   155
   Keep It Flexible   155
   Ensure Speed and Responsiveness   155
Conclusion   156
Endnotes   156

Chapter 13   Building an Internet Learning Solution   157
   Access Tools   158
   Internet Learning Applications   159
      Business Operations   159
      Content Management   162
      Delivery Management   164
      Learning Management Services   165
   The Network Infrastructure   166
   Cisco Case Study: A Role for Content-Delivery Networks in Internet Learning   167
      Challenge   168
      Solution   168
      Benefits and Results   169
   Collaborating to Create an Internet Solutions Architecture   171
   Conclusion   172

Chapter 14   Practitioners' Views on the Business Advantages of E-Learning   173
   Convergys Learning Solutions: A Perspective on Deployment   174
      Adopting Seamless Delivery Across the Enterprise   174
      Achieving Productivity Gains Through an Integrated Approach to E-Learning   175
      Viewing E-Learning as a Business Process Deployment   176
   ElementK: A Question of Leadership   176
   Cisco Communities: Building Customer Loyalty   179
      Knowledge Sharing Through Communities   180
      Knowledge Sharing Through Engaging Content   180
      Knowledge Sharing Through Events   180
      Justifying the Investment   181
      Conclusion   181

Epilogue   183

Index   185

Prologue

Hindsight Is 20/20

In 1997, much of the industry thought that e-learning was the latest training fad that would prove to be just as lackluster as some of the other fads of the past 20 years.

"Nothing can really replace the effectiveness of classroom learning" was a common statement, and an even more common belief. And there was some sound precedent for that position:

- Video-taped courses had proven to be a good bargain for purchasing agents but ineffective in actually training or even educating the large numbers of employees that were expected to flock to this medium. The libraries in corporate training facilities gathered dust quickly from lack of use.
- Laser Disc as a deployment medium was a short-lived, expensive technology alternative to the classroom. Its effectiveness, reach, and adoption underwhelmed even the most ardent proponents.
- CD-ROMs were a more effective medium for communicating to large, mobile audiences, but there was no good way to track usage or efficacy. Plus, there was no guarantee that they would work on my desktop. The combinations of sound card, video cards, and so on were not manageable for the producers. Hit or miss installations that sometimes caused PC failures ended up deterring learners from even trying, certainly from buying, this solution.

The list is much longer, but you get idea or you might remember the host of alternatives that held the learner hostage in classrooms and kept the trainers falling back into traditional solutions and historical methods of design and development.

Pragmatic visionaries (those who focus on possibilities that are only 12 months or less in the future) saw that the power of e-learning was the ubiquity of the Internet and importance of corporate intranets. There were fewer barriers (beyond the firewall issues) to participation, and there was a way to track every user's exact utilization. Plus, the network tools could collect enough metrics and statistics to fill volumes for the computationally driven. The only perceived problem was what browser people might use to access the content. It was naïve, maybe, but hopeful.

Traditionalists and those fiscally responsible for expense budgets saw yet another black training hole to throw money into with no way (again) of measuring successful learning, no way of judging business impact, and no hope establishing a true value proposition for investing more in e-training beyond the famous "you think training is expensive? Try ignorance!" Although that argument is a good attention getter, it has never won over any CFO making a budget decision.

Some of the early experiments in e-learning confirmed the pessimistic views. Traditionalists put their "courses online" and were disappointed in the student's reaction, being to e-read until they fell e-sleep. The best part of any "course" was the instructor (and the weakest link). Without an instructor, most course notes are lifeless and thus a bad choice for e-learning.

Thankfully, a number of people passionate about the business of learning kept on experimenting, executing, and progressing. The results were not failures because the only real failure is the inability to learn from an outcome. These folks persevered, found answers to the questions and solutions to problems, and then established routes to success and a wealth of information about how to do e-learning in ways (many ways) that have been successful on all levels: successful for the company, successful for the student/learner, and beneficial for the entire learning community, both private and public sectors.

A few of those successes are documented here as case studies. We hope you find them interesting and applicable to your business, institution, or learning environment.

Tom Kelly
August 2004

Introduction

E-learning equals productivity. If there were one theme that this book attempts to underscore, that would be it. A business case for e-learning is largely an effort to demonstrate the productivity advantages to an organization. Simply stated, productivity measures the output of an individual working in an organization against the input costs for supporting the individual in the organization.

Cisco internal analysis shows that every dollar spent on an e-learning portal for reseller development during fiscal year 2003 yielded $16 in earnings contribution for Cisco. (See Chapter 3, "E-Learning Under the Microscope," for details.) That's 16 times the value of every dollar invested in a single year. But how did that happen? Well, certainly not by throwing technology at the problem. Over the past seven years, Cisco has made a conscious effort to create an integrated productivity proposition using e-learning components and best practices.

Productivity is not just the domain of bean counters; the economic advantages reach far beyond the mere dollars and cents. Leaders who want to maximize the return on human capital, C-level decision makers who are concerned with the bottom line, and project managers who aim to bring short- and long-term projects under time and budget all benefit from productivity. Productivity not only contributes toward an organization's current bottom line, but it also determines the growth (and survival) of an entire ecosystem. An ecosystem includes those individuals who work outside the organization but have an impact on the overall performance of the organization (for example, resellers, suppliers, customers, and consultants).

In their quest for productivity, organizations might reap glory from committing to the mundane. Review a simple illustration of managing employee travel and reimbursement online as having positive impact on productivity. By making their air, hotel, and rental car reservations online, employees circumvent the need for an official travel agent or a travel department. In certain cases, even administrative staff is spared the back and forth that transpires while fine-tuning an itinerary. On the back end, requesting reimbursement of expenses online reduces the time and improves the timeliness of filing, reviewing, auditing, and disbursement. Trivial as it might appear, in addition to saving the company time and money, such process improvement increases employee control of the process and reduces employee frustration with delays. The cumulative effect of such productivity efforts over the long run cannot be discounted in an organization.

When process improvement takes effect, an organization stands to gain more than merely savings in time and money. Process improvements set individuals, their customers, their providers, and therefore an entire ecosystem on the path to productivity. The autonomy and speed of decision making sets high-performing groups apart. Although an organization driven by productivity expects its work force to do more with less, it also empowers its work force to assume risks and demonstrate entrepreneurial initiative. The higher level of satisfaction within the work force sets the collective talent in the desired direction. How can a team ever win without empowering the individuals?

What Is This Book About?

The purpose of this book is to describe communication, collaboration, training, and assessment efforts within any organization that would enable any work force to rise above its current performance level. The model presented in the book is a results-oriented approach to professional development of individuals. It is not just an abstract thought, but a construct based on empirical evidence and proven practice.

This book demonstrates that e-learning works best when a combination of e-communication, e-training, and e-assessment tools is utilized in a networked environment. Individual growth and development with the approach discussed in the book far exceeds the advantages of having only one or two of these tools in place. In other words, there is a synergistic value in having these specific learning components operate in tandem. Ignoring the synergy of an integrated approach leads to only marginal success with Internet-based learning efforts. That lack of synergy may even help explain the less than stellar results from e-learning in some quarters.

How Is This Book Relevant?

The logical implications of the approach are not limited to just multinational Fortune 500 enterprises, but pertain even to the small businesses. Consider an individual who is beginning an accounting or bookkeeping practice. Would it not be valuable for such an individual to have access to a source for the latest research and findings on tax laws and changes? And would this entrepreneur not benefit from interaction with peers at an accounting association during the course of the year to exchange best practices? Would it not be valuable for the individual to have training on new techniques and tools at least once a year? And would it also not be valuable to pass exams or certifications that demonstrate recently acquired skills so that he can serve his clients in those areas? Most of all, would it not work to the individuals' advantage if they could access all the communication, collaboration, learning, and certification over an online database instead of having to travel, having to take time out of a busy practice, or having to be away from customers for a length of time? Questions such as these are discussed throughout the book in the context of business organizations.

Stretch the concept further by discussing a more far-fetched example from a social situation: AIDS prevention in Africa. If a local physician had access to the Internet, would it not benefit her clients if she had the latest approaches to prevention techniques from a database that stores best practices from the worldwide experience in prevention? What if the physician could take training courses on treatment and prevention from some of the experts located worldwide over the Internet? And ask and post questions ... and receive replies? What if all caseworkers in Africa had to pass an international exam to ensure consistent delivery of care across different nations? Such an endeavor would not just create better caseworkers, it would also likely improve patient care, save families, and contribute to the survival of entire societies.

The possible benefits are endless if we train people using an integrated productivity approach. The impact is evident on an entire ecosystem. At the risk of sounding trite, we reiterate a cliché lest we forget: Knowledge means power (and that power includes healing). And unleashing that power through e-learning with a systematic approach has demonstrated success for Cisco. We are confident that it will for others who adopt it as well.

More than deployment of technology, e-learning is about a process that meets learner needs with relevant content and with technology-enabled tools that are convenient in the learner's context. Never before have issues of work-force development been addressed with a tool as ubiquitous and versatile as the Internet is today.

What Is the Difference Between Productivity, Performance, and Profitability?

Dividing the revenues of an organization or an ecosystem by the number of workers has been the simplest metric for measuring productivity. With stable or declining revenues, certain managers are tempted to reduce the work force to demonstrate stronger productivity numbers. A complementary measure of productivity improvement is an increasing or stable contribution margin. If increasing productivity is not backed with a solid gross margin, the productivity gains might be attributed to a function of work-force reduction rather than work-force development.

On the other hand, performance and profitability measure the quality and effectiveness of the output. Meeting company objectives with high customer satisfaction ratings demonstrates high performance on the part of a work force. After the year 2000, an increasing emphasis on generating profitability for the organization was evident in the business environment. An effort to improve productivity, within a context of performance and profitability, can generate genuine value for an organization or an ecosystem. In the larger context, productivity, performance, and profitability should play in concert much like the three valves on a saxophone—in harmony to create a coherent effect.

Who Is the Book For?

The book is intended for chief learning officers, executive directors, project managers, business managers, IT managers, consultants, and training managers who are responsible for improving organizational productivity through the use of Internet learning. The book is as much a tool for organizational development as it is for work-force development.

Utilizing Internet learning does not mean mere conversion of face-to-face courses to web-based courses. Instead, it involves a broader view of e-learning. This is why the book provides guidelines to change agents in organizations on why-to's and how-to's.

We encourage you to adopt the practices described in this book into your plans and projects. We have covered certain planning models in the book. If you are a consultant, integrate the planning model into your consulting approach. We invite you to review the checklists that are provided in the book and incorporate some of the ideas into your project-planning efforts. The writing that follows is based on success. Because at the time we were more concerned with getting the job done and being successful at it instead of writing a book about it later, not all of what we recommend here will stand the academic test of defensibility; however, it provides insight into our experience that has helped deliver results at Cisco.

The recurring sections on "Hindsight Is 20/20" underscore Tom Kelly's observations based on his more than 20 years of experience with learning and management. These shaded sections are candid conversations that offer a perspective based on first-hand experience.

What Makes Us So Sure?

Not all that is described here happened by design. Often, the best strategies evolve in response to unforeseen situations rather than a rational assessment of the environment. The approaches evolved during some difficult times that Cisco had to endure. Attempting to increase productivity in difficult times taught us to be innovative.

The book has not been written to demonstrate that Cisco has it all figured out, but instead to document our experience as we muddled through when responding to the changing business around us. We share the thoughts, experiences, and ideas presented in the following chapters with the hope that they will prove to be valuable tools for you. The information presented here might help to reduce your organization's or ecosystem's learning curve as you pursue your Internet learning efforts. And if indeed you reduce the trial and error in your e-learning efforts as a result of reading this book, our writing endeavor will have been well worth the effort.

Topics Covered in This Book

Part I: Understanding the Business Impact of E-Learning:

Chapter 1, "Vaulted: From the Classroom to the Boardroom," discusses some of the compelling reasons that made e-learning a priority for Cisco (and its ecosystem).

Chapter 2, "Internet Learning: A Productivity Tool," addresses the question "Is e-learning a feel-good experience?"

Chapter 3, "E-Learning Under the Microscope," discusses ways to assess the value on investment in e-learning.

Part II: Business Success with E-Learning:

Chapter 4, "BearingPoint Makes a Grand Slam with Internet Learning: A Case Study," reviews the experience of BearingPoint to demonstrate how a company used e-learning to transform its business practices within a short amount of time.

Chapter 5, "Learner Driven at the University of Toyota: Pioneers of Just-in-Time Advocate 'Hands-On' Skills," reviews the practices of just-in-time training at the University of Toyota.

Chapter 6, "E-Learning Goes Global: Networking Academy Transforms Lives," presents a global approach to deploying Internet learning to change thousands of lives.

Chapter 7, "Targeted Learning: Are You *Indeed* Ready?" discusses the approach Cisco utilized to targeted learning for its sales force development.

Chapter 8, "Productivity in the Extended Enterprise: Internet Learning Offers a Competitive Edge with Channel Partners," demonstrates how Internet learning can turn anytime-anyplace learning into a competitive advantage.

Chapter 9, "Picking a Networking Dream Team," discusses the merger between Global One and Sita/Equant to highlight the value of technology integration and talent to strategic priorities.

Chapter 10, "Certifications as a Branding Tool: Sponsoring a Certification Program," provides a model for creating a certification program to encourage common practices and equitable compensation across an ecosystem.

Part III: Deploying Your E-Learning Efforts: Best Practices

Chapter 11, "The Building Blocks," discusses the steps that you can follow as you plan your next move with Internet learning.

Chapter 12, "Organizing an Internet Learning Initiative," covers specific action items necessary to complete an e-learning implementation. The recommendations are based on Cisco best practices with e-learning deployment and are applicable to organizations both large and small.

Chapter 13, "Building an Internet Learning Solution," presents a checklist that you can follow when thinking through all the technological components of an Internet learning architecture. The checklist offers planners and decision makers an understanding of how each of the components might affect an e-learning effort within an organization. The chapter concludes with a case study on the deployment of e-learning architecture.

Chapter 14, "Practitioners' Views on the Business Advantages of E-Learning," is based on discussions with practitioners and explores how they think e-learning might impact organizations as a strategic tool in the future.

CHAPTER 1

Vaulted: From the Classroom to the Boardroom

On February 5, 2001, Cisco Systems reported what were in many respects historic results. Cisco missed analysts' earnings estimates, and Wall Street marked the end of the tech-driven boom years of the 1990s. After nine years of expansion, the technology sector, and eventually the rest of the U.S. economy, headed into a recession.

In essence, the script had been rewritten. Companies that had been flush with growth were now fighting to survive. From a time when investment dollars were chasing bright ideas, the markets had moved to an environment in which investors were seeking accountability. The question was not how to do more; it was how do you do more with much less? After years of keeping revenue ahead of everything, analysts, executives, and shareholders realized that productivity, cash flow, and profitability concerns eclipsed all else.

A Once-in-a-Hundred-Year Flood: After the Bubble

The months after that fateful February were marked by high hopes for e-learning (which was a vital Cisco asset). Infrastructure was still important, but applications ruled. Customers had to figure out how to leverage their investment in technology through solutions. In a "show-me" economy, Cisco was not only expected to show customers that the applications would change the way businesses do business, but Cisco was also expected to demonstrate financial success with those applications to leverage its network to increase its productivity and profitability and to streamline its business process. Cisco was expected to walk the talk. E-learning was too critical an application to be left for the training department alone. It now belonged in the boardroom as a strategy for business and a tactic for profitability.

On the first floor of Building 8 on the Cisco campus, John Chambers, the CEO of Cisco, conducted a number of video events simulcast over the web. The message from the CEO was consistent to each employee. No organizational filters or distortions altered his message. Some logged in to the presentations from their desks, and those working remotely pulled the presentation up on their PCs from home; still others, who were in a different time zone, accessed it on demand later. The message was direct and one on one, from the CEO to each employee.

There was an advantage to such one-on-one communication. Only the CEO had the credibility to quell rumors, boost morale, and point to the light at the end of the tunnel. An organization of more than 40,000 employees had to be motivated to pursue organizational success. The changing face of the business climate was to be understood and embraced by all the employees. The video presentations outlined the goals and the direction for the company and the priorities for cooperation and personal success. Employees reeling from the economic blows hung on to each word looking for answers about how to survive and thrive in a changing world.

Cisco had to be transformed: Expenses had to be curtailed, budgets had to be cut, costs had to be reigned in, inventories had to be scaled, and customers still had to be served. Disparate efforts across the company had to centralize at a higher level than before to avoid duplication and waste. You can do more with less waste.

Enabled communication remained the lifeblood of Cisco in the course of these changes. Senior leadership clarified what was on their mind, including leadership's agenda, what the shareholders expected, what to brace for next, and how to cope with the changes. The constant communication kept the organization connected when times conspired to tear it apart. Cisco leveraged its e-learning tools to secure the fabric of the organization. After three years of investment and implementation, it was during these days of adversity that e-learning went prime time at Cisco.

The Three Waves of E-Learning at Cisco

The pioneering e-learning effort required years of fine-tuning and adjustment before mainstream acceptance at Cisco. E-mail was available in the late 1970s but could not be sent between systems until the late 1980s. E-mail, as a communications tool, was used for 10 years in research settings before early users adopted it, and another 3 to 5 years before the mainstream users adopted it. At Cisco, generating productivity from Internet learning applications has been an evolutionary process. Since 1997, e-learning has evolved in phases or, what is often referred to as, "waves" of adoption. Throughout this book, the terms *Internet learning* and *e-learning* are used interchangeably.

Table 1-1   Three Waves of E-Learning Adoption Based on Cisco Deployment Experience

	Wave 1 (1997–1999)	**Wave 2 (2000–2001)**	**Wave 3 (2002+)**
Financial benefit	$24-million annual benefit	$31-million annual benefit	$133-million annual benefit
Business benefit (competitive advantage)	Reduced time and expenses Faster time to competency	Competitive advantage with reseller partners Greater accountability	Improved reporting and skill management Higher productivity
Applications (scope of capabilities)	Video on demand Learning management system	Virtual classroom Content portal by role Global streaming network	Learning objects Global e-learning platform CDN deployment
Impact on people (breadth of capabilities)	Sales and manufacturing	Channel partners and engineering	Customers and other groups (legal, finance, and so on)

During the first phase from 1997 to 1999, the focus was primarily on providing training through electronic distribution. Faster time to competence and reduced travel expenses were the driving motivators. Although Cisco recorded an annual internal benefit of $24 million, the days were still early for e-learning in the company.

This first wave focused on sales and manufacturing within Cisco as the key target audience for e-learning. The primary reason for selecting sales and manufacturing was the readiness and willingness to adopt alternative training techniques. The tools that were most readily deployed to support this effort were video on demand, self-paced lessons, and a learning management system.

The premier networking certification, *Cisco Certified Internetwork Expert (CCIE)*, predates this first wave. During this first-wave phase, however, Cisco also launched mid-career and entry-level certifications to broaden the appeal of the

Chapter 1: Vaulted: From the Classroom to the Boardroom

program for candidates seeking stepping-stones. The Cisco certification program achieved its early success because of its adoption among the sales force and Cisco reseller partners, also referred to as *channel partners*.

The second wave followed from 2000 to 2001. During this time, Cisco introduced two learning portals: The *Field E-Learning Connection (FELC)* was introduced for the sales force, and the *Partner E-Learning Connection (PEC)* was launched to meet the training needs of the channel partners. With the launch of the portals, the emphasis on Internet learning applications expanded beyond training toward communication. Testing was an occasional element but not an integrated component. During this period, Cisco assessed an annual benefit of $31 million from investment in training and communication.[1]

The benefits from the Cisco Career Certifications program accrued in the form of customer loyalty and industry recognition. By May 2001, nearly a quarter of a million networking professionals worldwide had acquired a Cisco certification. Industry analysts recognized Cisco certifications as the fastest-growing certification program in the IT sector. Customers had begun to rely on the program to identify talent for supporting their networks. Nearly 10 percent of the Cisco-certified individuals in 2001 were Cisco employees, with another estimated 30 percent being channel partners. The remaining 60 percent included Cisco customers, independent consultants, and IT professionals worldwide.

Besides the certifications program, Cisco enhanced its assessment component through the introduction of online testing. Online testing was targeted for use within Cisco sales force and channel to test competencies on certain skill sets. Besides certifications, the online testing has become a means for sales managers to ensure that planning, design, and support teams working on customer networks possess necessary understanding to perform the required tasks.

The learning components coalesced in the third wave, where communication, training, and assessment operated in sync. The organization had realized the value of e-enabling communication, training, and assessment. Employee rewards were tied to online testing and certification accomplishment. Electronically distributed certification-training materials were available for learners to use. The most recent information about product, technologies, and services from Cisco were available on the web through online courses, video-on-demand segments, and white papers.

The productivity benefits to Cisco reached $133 million in fiscal year 2002, a net increase of $100 million. The surge in productivity might be attributed in part to the synergy within the components of Internet learning. An improved adoption rate among learners and improvement in skill management and distribution tools were evident. On the certifications front, more than 400,000 individuals had acquired a Cisco certification, and performance-based simulation questions were now a regular feature in certification testing. On the learning portals, 78 percent of the sales force was acquiring 80 percent of the information it needed from the sales portal. The organization, as a whole, was conducting 400 video-on-demand presentations each month and more than 40 live video broadcasts each month.[2]

The e-learning initiative focused on leveraging employee knowledge and skills through Internet application solutions. It ultimately promised that e-learning solutions could thrive and generate productivity benefits.

The Productivity Imperative

In 2004, the mood was cautious and optimistic, but muted. However, while waiting for business and IT spending to pick up, Cisco did manage market-share growth. The company bounced back practicing what it preached: Leverage the Internet to change the way of doing business.

During this time, the expectation of employee productivity at Cisco remained ambitious and its pursuit relentless. This resulted in a 25 percent to 30 percent productivity increase in 24 months. Cisco leadership remained committed to increasing future productivity through Internet business solutions and employee empowerment. The cornerstone of education and experience is communications, training, and assessment delivered over the Internet: e-learning.

The Net Impact of Productivity

A focus on generating productivity set the stage for understanding and using the Internet as a resource. A study conducted in 2001, called Net Impact, assessed the productivity advantages from existing and planned Internet applications at $528 billion for the U.S. economy alone. (See Figure 1-1.) For Europe, the benefits were estimated at $148 billion for organizations that participated in the study. The monetary benefits would accrue through 2010, when all these applications are expected to be complete.[3]

Chapter 1: Vaulted: From the Classroom to the Boardroom

Figure 1-1   The Net Impact Study

The Net Impact Study—Internet Business Solutions

...a major wake-up call for most large enterprises... network infrastructure is directly tied to the ability to gain competitive advantage in the marketplace today and in the future

David Passmore, Burton Group
July 2001

The Net Impact Study

- Co-operative effort between Cisco Systems and researchers at UC Berkeley. The Brookings Institution and Momentum Research Group

- Participants:
  2065 U.S. organizations
  534 U.K., French and German organizations

- Study results reflect direct customer experiences

Net Impact Results

- 61% of U.S. businesses have adopted any internet business solutions

- U.S. organizations expect to save $528 billion cumulatively on current IBS initiatives

- By 2010 network-enabled applications could account for 48% of the projected productivity increase in the U.S. economy

---

Researchers of the study at the University of California, Berkeley, the Brookings Institution, and Momentum Research Group had for the first time quantified the extent to which organizations might be able to benefit from cost savings or revenue increases through the adoption of Internet business solutions. For the purposes of the study, Internet business solutions were defined as IT initiatives that leverage the Internet with networking, computing hardware or software for streamlining business processes, or cultivating opportunities. More than 2500 companies from the United States and Europe participated in the study.

The study clearly demonstrated that economies globally still have a lot of room for productivity growth—and when there is genuine productivity growth in economies, stock markets register and reflect the gains eventually. The opportunities appear even more promising than reported, however, because only 60 percent of the U.S. businesses and 44 percent of European businesses reported any ongoing applications. What if the remaining organizations decide to leverage Internet business solutions? What if those that are currently generating the savings go beyond the first round of business solutions to another wave of Internet applications? The estimated savings are a striking $1.4 trillion over a 10-year period if all businesses in the United States implement Internet business solutions—better than any stimulus package the government can offer.

The Net Impact study offered insight on productivity based on Internet applications that offer promise of generating true value for businesses worldwide. The study indicated three types of productivity advantages accruing to organizations as a result of Internet business solutions:

- **Productivity gains through cost savings**—In the United States, organizations that have adopted Internet applications realized cost savings at an average of 2 percent to 4 percent per year with an expected savings of 5 percent to 9 percent on average annually.

  In Europe, organizations that have adopted Internet applications realized cost savings at an average of 2 percent to 6 percent each year with an expected savings of 5 percent to 16 percent on average each year.

- **Productivity gains through revenue**—Internet applications help attract and retain customers over the long term. More than 50 percent of the organizations involved in the study reported attracting customers as a result of their Internet applications. Another 50 percent reported improving customer satisfaction as a result of these applications.

- **Productivity gains through compounding**—Organizations that adopted two or more Internet business solutions for business applications realized double the cost savings, a clear indication of synergy across applications.

Employee Productivity Through Internet Learning

In economic terms, productivity is defined as the rate at which goods or services are produced, as measured by output per unit of labor. In today's high-tech economy, however, clear and consistent communication and the flow of knowledge and information within an organization often profoundly affect a company's ability to be productive. A better-trained and better-informed employee returns the investment in training and development multiple times over through improved performance for the organization.

To create high achievers—not only for the company, but also for the resellers—Cisco created (in the year 2000) an e-learning portal for 400 worldwide reseller partners and another for 4000 systems engineers. The users included

Chapter 1: Vaulted: From the Classroom to the Boardroom

groups that ensured not only the sale of Cisco products but also the deployment of those products. (See Table 1-2.) The lines between information and training began to blur as users began to receive just-in-time information on products and solutions from the learning portal. Of all users, 75 percent rated high satisfaction with the learning tool, and 90 percent reported that they would recommend the learning portal to others.[4]

Table 1-2   FELC and PEC Figures

FELC Monthly Users (Cisco Sales)	
Americas	872
Asia Pac	2013
EMEA	4026
Japan	866
U.S.	13,967
Total	22,744
PEC Monthly Users (Partners)	
Americas	7390
Asia Pac	12,640
EMEA	20,966
Japan	914
U.S.	37,434
Total	80,618

The more learners that used the e-learning portal, the higher they reported their satisfaction with the tool. The use resulted in *Sales & Marketing Management* magazine rating the Cisco sales team as the "best-trained sales force" in the United States across all industries in 2002.[5] In the fourth quarter of fiscal 2002 alone, Cisco achieved a 40 percent to 60 percent cost savings through increased use of e-learning over in-class training.[6]

The return on investment (ROI) analysis conducted on the e-learning portal for resellers, called Partner E-learning Connection (PEC), has validated the business benefits of the portal. For each dollar spent on the PEC in fiscal year 2003, the e-learning portal yielded $16 of value for Cisco. (See Chapter 3, "E-learning Under the Microscope," for more details on the analysis.)

A C-Level Perspective: Banking on the Knowledge Worker

As noted earlier, the problem of doing more with less leveraged the idea that you could use Internet applications to sustain productivity. So how do C-level decision makers, such as a *chief information officers (CIOs)*, respond to a call for "doing more with less?" The answer is simple: by leveraging Internet applications to sustain productivity gains over the long run and by cultivating knowledge workers within the organization. A *knowledge worker* is one who efficiently and effectively delivers mission-critical applications and projects for the organization. Research, such as the Net Impact study, and experience has shown that 2 percent to 6 percent annual productivity gains are entirely attainable over the course of the current decade.

Fiscally minded organizations seek to increase their economic return on employee investment. The talent needed to implement, integrate, and perform critical projects has always been at a premium. In an economic slowdown, workers are expected to perform with even fewer resources. In turn, these workers need increased information, authority, and skills development to keep pace with trends, technologies, and innovations around them. Knowledge workers have a way of returning rich dividends to companies that invest in them. These dividends include the following:

- **Reduced cost and time**—Demonstrating high levels of competence, knowledge workers reduce the cost of maintenance and time to market with development and implementation. Qualified expertise on project teams naturally helps a company reduce the time and cost required to meet project- or product-development goals.

- **Increased success with customers**—Organizations involved in consulting and reselling, with highly skilled individuals on staff, often enjoy a competitive advantage when competing for projects.

- **Revenue generation**—Value-added products and services improve revenue stream for those in the business of reselling, consulting, manufacturing, and information services. Teams that design, develop, and deliver such products and services form a revenue-generating source for companies.[7]

Chapter 1: Vaulted: From the Classroom to the Boardroom

The Promise of E-Learning: Learning in Lean Times

If during a slower business climate organizations focus on improving productivity, investments in developing knowledge workers follow. However, with cost pressures, organizations often must cut the budgets that support the learning needs of their employees. With limited budgets for skill development, decision makers tend to assess learning options on the basis of time, cost, and learning effectiveness.

Hindsight Is 20/20: How Is E-Learning Strategic?

Training has been around for years and has never been an integral or strategic part of most product launches, much less integral or strategic to the business. Why is e-learning going to be any different?

E-learning, because it is implemented on an intranet or the Internet, offers something no other training, communication, or education tool ever has: accountability on a grand scale. Getting training information into the hands of users has traditionally been accomplished in a number of ways: videotapes, laser discs, multimedia CD-ROMs, books, white papers, PowerPoint slides, and many other deployment vehicles. Until e-learning, however, it was impossible effectively or affordably to hold the learner accountable for using the product to actually learn anything, whether it was skills or knowledge based. We measured how many products were sent out or how many were purchased, but never got a good idea of the usage, effectiveness, or the impact of all that effort. We did not even know whether we had chosen the most effective media for the subject or the specific audience.

Today, however, we can test each individual on each module or chapter. We can report progress and can analyze data to determine whether the content is flawed, the media is inadequate, or the test item itself is invalid. We can hold learners accountable for what they are supposed to know and the authors and developers accountable for the content quality, and we can determine whether we have used the best media for a specific topic and for a specific audience.

For example, the Cisco Networking Academies are globally deployed in public schools, colleges, and universities. Within the academies are more than 300,000 students in more than 11,000 schools in more than 150 countries using the same online content (in 9 languages) for learning and testing. More than 40,000 tests are taken every day. Scores and trends are analyzed, and then flaws in content, instruction, or testing are identified and fixed. Continual improvement based on results and hard data on a global scale, and information that is not possible to gather in traditional classroom settings, makes this system of learning more accountable, hence more effective.

The other advantage e-learning offers is maintainability. What is the difference between a book, videotape, and a CD-ROM? When it comes to edits, changes, and updates to existing products, there is little or no difference. All three take weeks or months to edit, update, republish, and redistribute. The cost in time and reproduction dollars (or euros, or yen) is incredibly high (not to mention repeated translation costs). With e-learning products, maintenance is easier, faster, and dramatically cheaper (when compared to the total cost of publishing and factoring in the impact of immediate deployment).

Internet Learning: Options and Alternatives

The impact of learning and work-force development on productivity has often been difficult to demonstrate in the business world. Many decision makers remain unsure exactly how to guarantee that their investments in learning opportunities will be worthwhile. As a result, a deliberate approach to assessing training is critical for ensuring a return or value on investment. Organizations are faced with a multitude of options, including those shown in Figure 1-2. Just picking an option might not suffice, however; that option must be backed with a comprehensive system.

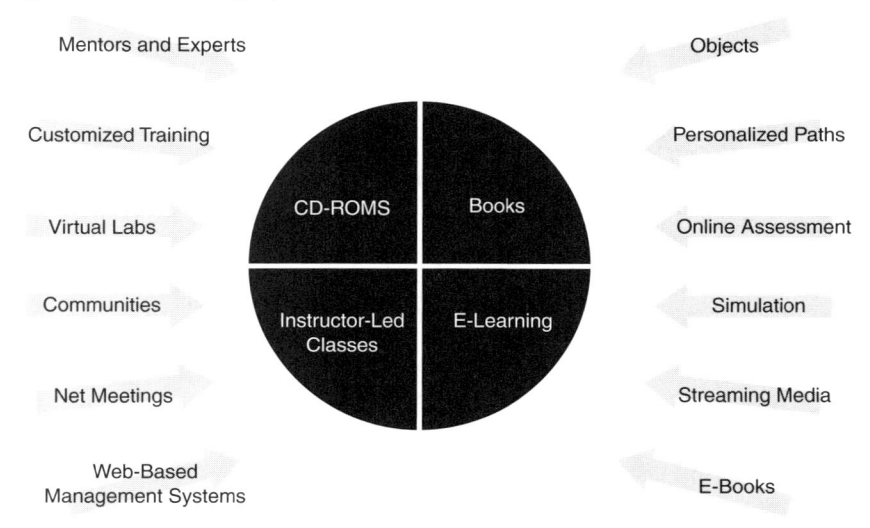

Figure 1-2 *Learning Options*

- Mentors and Experts
- Customized Training
- Virtual Labs
- Communities
- Net Meetings
- Web-Based Management Systems
- CD-ROMS
- Books
- Instructor-Led Classes
- E-Learning
- Objects
- Personalized Paths
- Online Assessment
- Simulation
- Streaming Media
- E-Books

The following list describes common types of training or learning available in the industry:

- **Traditional training**—Traditional, instructor-led (face-to-face) classroom instruction has been the mainstay of most organizational learning. For decades, classroom instruction generated one-on-one relationships between the instructor and the students, stimulated group discussion among peers, and supported an interactive forum for discourse. The disadvantage from the employer's perspective has always been the cost of travel and lodging (and, most importantly, the time employees spend away from work).[8]

- **E-learning**—E-learning is available in a variety of types and forms. Instructor-led, simulations, and self-paced e-learning are a couple of examples. E-learning is often defined as e-training. Such a definition is limiting in that it portrays e-learning as little more than the components of the traditional classroom converted into electronic delivery. Empirical results on learning and credentialing show that effectiveness of such e-learning compares favorably with face-to-face instruction. Most learners are likely to choose e-learning as a substitute to face-to-face instruction when economic resources are limited.[8]

E-learning can be delivered in the following formats:

- *Modular learning*—Modular learning enables an individual to learn in chunks that are most relevant. Practice exercises, virtual mentoring, online lectures, and remote labs and simulations can be delivered to the desktop to enable learners to tailor their learning based on specific needs.[9]
- *Blended learning*—Blended learning offers the option to integrate traditional instruction and electronic self-paced learning. With an instructor or an online mentor at their disposal, learners can pursue learning secure in the knowledge that a trained expert will evaluate performance and offer relevant feedback along the way.[10]

Although many are convinced that e-learning presents potential opportunities, converting learning into measurable organizational success has proved clumsy. Many managers across a variety of organizations exhibit a broad understanding of e-learning, but few have been able to incorporate Internet learning robustly into a strategy for productivity gains. Deploying Internet learning with a focus on improving organizational success requires a purposeful "road map"—an integrated plan that extends beyond the immediate benefits of e-learning. Without such a plan, e-learning might ultimately prove to be only a cost-saving device or, at worst, an instructional experiment.

Hindsight Is 20/20: Will It Cut the Muster?

The classroom is the only really effective way to learn, isn't it?

No, emphatically untrue.

Good instructors make classroom learning as good as it can be, but it is not the best way to learn or teach every subject. It is the most common way to teach most subjects, but far from the only effective way. Where is the best place to learn about golf? What is the best way to teach astronomy? Does the best learning happen with the instructor lecturing or during discussion with other students? My freshman psychology class was composed of 1200 students in a very large auditorium with 10 televisions on the walls that showed the instructor on stage 100 yards away. A sound instructional model?

Chapter 1: Vaulted: From the Classroom to the Boardroom

We learned more during 40 hours as a counselor's helper at a youth detention center than we did in 60 hours of lecture in that room. In an industrialized society with goals focused on standardized curricula and testing, the classroom was a viable solution. In the school system of my youth, that "sage on the stage" was our portal into the world of history, math, political science, chemistry, and business management. That was the time that came before 7×24 access to the largest library in the history of the world: the Internet. Today, you can find out almost anything you want to know, about almost any topic that piques your curiosity, by accessing the web through any number of devices or portals.

Even Internet games teach players how to play, or how to use the "graffiti" of your newest handheld PDA, or how to build and manage an amusement park business, or how to manage resources to attain some desired goal (such as the Sims, Warcraft, Roller Coaster, Sim City).

There are lots of ways to teach and to learn. No one method works for everyone, every job, or every industry. The learning industry has begun to awaken to the fact that learning is an individual experience. Whether on your own or in the classroom, learning is a personal experience that should be tailored to make the experience enjoyable, effective, and satisfying for the learner.

The relevant questions that educators must answer include

- Which medium is best to convey knowledge to a specific audience regarding a specific topic?
- What kind of connectivity and access do learners have?
- When do the learners need access to course material?
- At what stage is information and training relevant to the learners?
- Should training be offered at the beginning of the class or staged along a development path?

Some topics are best covered in the classroom, and some people learn best in a traditional classroom setting; however, a number of constraints apply to classroom learning that prevent it from scaling, including the number of classrooms and instructors, the location, the number of students necessary to justify the business expenses of the classroom instruction, and the time away from family and job.

> Even if you still believe that classroom learning is best, do not make the mistake of thinking that it is the only education model for your organization. Traditional classroom education is being supplemented more and more with nontraditional conveyance of knowledge. Younger generations, especially, *expect* to rely on other tools than just the instructor to gather knowledge (and expect to be able to do so on their own schedule). These young people are used to access and control when it comes to information, communication, and training. They are now demanding it in the workplace, not just in the mall, their classrooms, Starbucks, and their homes.

End Notes

[1] Kelly, Tom and Diane Bauer. "Managing Intellectual Capital at Cisco," Handbook of Knowledge Management Volume. Edited by C. W. Holsapple, Springer-Verlag, December 2002.

[2] ibid

[3] Brookings Institution and Momentum Research Group. "The Net Impact Study," Cooperative effort with Cisco, July 2001.

[4] Galagan, Patricia. "Delta Force," *Training* Magazine, Lakewood Publications, May 2002.

[5] ibid.

[6] ibid.

[7] ibid.

[8] Nanjiani, Nader. "Talent for Turbulent Times," *Certifications* Magazine, MediaTec Publishing, May 2002.

[9] Nanjiani, Nader. "Climbing the Certifications Ladder," *Certifications* Magazine, MediaTec Publishing, September 2002.

[10] ibid.

[11] ibid.

[12] ibid.

CHAPTER 2

INTERNET LEARNING— A PRODUCTIVITY TOOL

Organizational decision makers who strive to make their companies more productive are incorporating Internet learning. If a company's productivity improves through enhanced employee learning, it stands to reason that the adoption of an e-learning program should positively affect that organization's productivity levels. This chapter aims to address the role of Internet learning in increasing organizational productivity.

Charting a Course

In an integrated learning effort aimed at generating productivity, a company will choose e-learning learning system applications and services that address elements such as knowledge, understanding, and skills. As shown in Figure 2-1, a comprehensive Internet learning system includes the following components:

1 **E-communication**—The e-communication program should incorporate the use of a variety of learning portals including live and on-demand video, audio content, knowledge-management tools, just-in-time information tools, websites, e-mail, electronic libraries and archives, electronic conferencing, and "anytime- anyplace" access tools.

2 **E-training**—The e-training program is often formal and self-paced, and it often provides modular learning opportunities, a learning-management system, relevant content, and a structured approach.

3 **E-assessment**—Participants should be able to test their knowledge through online exams and proctored exams, and they should be able to get acquired skills validated through certification.

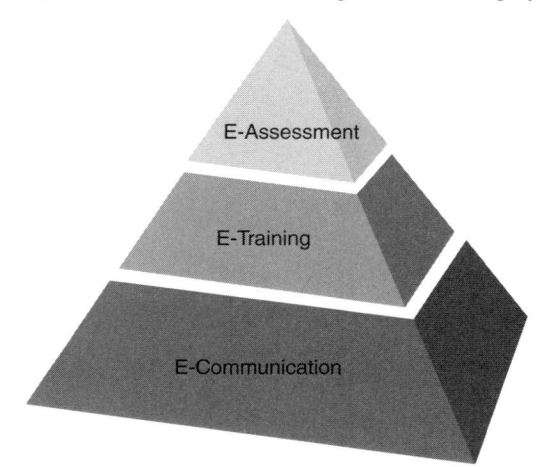

Figure 2-1 Comprehensive Internet Learning or E-Learning System

E-Assessment

E-Training

E-Communication

The components of a successful e-learning program can be viewed as a pyramid: As the most familiar and widely used, e-communication represents the first tier of the pyramid, offering the access that a work force needs for empowerment and knowledge sharing. The development of skills through e-training represents the second tier, where the level of use is less widespread and more specific and structured. The third tier, e-assessment, represents the apex of the pyramid, because the assessment component of this integrated learning system is the area in which retention and performance can be validated against established benchmarks.

Synergy

So where is the synergy in bringing assessment, training, and communication under the umbrella of a productivity effort? The advantage is in the skilled use of knowledge that learners demonstrate as a result. Imagine an experienced project engineer sharing experience on the job by using e-communication tools to create presentations or videos on demand for customers or peers. This application is followed up with specific formal training, using self-paced modules. After an individual has acquired substantial new knowledge, that individual may feel ready to take on more responsibilities. To determine whether learning has indeed taken place, the individual pursues a certification. Such demonstration of learning, retention, and performance is not possible unless all three components align in an integrated e-learning system.

A work force must be able to access personalized learning tools that will lead to greater productivity. Envisioning an Internet learning system as a pyramid allows an organization to think through the components and successfully implement the program. It is the integration and intersection of these components that generates measurable productivity leaps for any organization.

Although the discussion on the surface appears to address larger enterprises, it is important to note that an integrated approach to e-learning is applicable to smaller organizations as well. Where building certain components in-house might not make sense for smaller organizations, smaller companies might be able to tap into the resources of others. Not all components of e-learning need to be created internally or purchased; some or all of the components may be bought or outsourced.

A Matter of Semantics

For the purposes of this book, Internet learning and e-learning are one and the same. In a productivity pyramid metaphor, e-training refers to electronic delivery of training content. Others refer to any form of electronic delivery as e-learning instead of e-training. Semantics aside, the Cisco approach is about combining readiness, skills development, and skills assessment into a single system. Whether it is referred to as e-learning or Internet learning, what matters is that it will struggle for success unless all necessary components are in place.

Hindsight Is 20/20: Training Versus E-Learning

How does education and training differ from e-learning?

E-learning provides the means to deliver education and training (and other kinds of) content. Education and training are structured learning experiences that change the knowledge or skill level of the learner.

E-learning represents the many ways to get the content to the learners. It is *not* just a technology.

It changes how and what we say, to whom, and when. We cannot simply put existing content "on the web" and expect it to have any meaningful learning impact. E-learning changes education and training methodologies because it changes how content is organized, delivered, received, and possibly even assimilated.

E-mail changed how we communicate because it changed how we connect to each other. It has changed the ease, frequency, and even the quality of that communication. In the same respect, voicemail has changed telephone communications. E-learning has a similar effect on education and training concepts and content, and possibly on the learner communities themselves.

The Scope of Productivity Improvements

Productivity changes are often measured in terms of what they mean for the organization. In such analyses, organizations often cannot or do not calculate the benefits downstream to customers and upstream to suppliers. With skills and learners in focus, managers who deploy effective Internet learning systems can achieve an impact beyond the reach of their organizations. In this scenario, productivity can be viewed as a longer, connected chain of people who have a broader business impact.

To make product lines successful, many organizations have to increase the skills and knowledge level throughout a value chain rather than just within the organization. For example, an equipment reseller can help its customers improve productivity while also helping to improve the productivity of the equipment manufacturer downstream and upstream.

The art and science of implementing an integrated learning strategy to improve a company's productivity often lies in looking beyond the current definitions of Internet learning. Success lies in focusing on new measurement tools and new metrics.

Collectively, the three components—communications, training, and assessment—nurture a system that allows organizational competence and workforce output to be measured and enhanced. In 2003, Cisco Systems realized a $142-million financial benefit from this type of comprehensive e-learning program. In addition, employees who change jobs can acquire the necessary competence up to 40 percent faster through e-learning than employees who use the classroom to acquire the same knowledge or skills.

The Advantages from an Employer Perspective

From an employer perspective, each e-learning component corresponds to an organizational advantage. Following are advantages:

- **E-communication** translates into strategic alignment. The use of e-communication enables strategic alignment between organizational priorities and the work force within an organization or ecosystem through knowledge sharing. The virtual intimacy and proximity created through presentations over Internet video not only helps to level the playing field between headquarter-based employees and remote employees, but it also allows a sense of connectedness in mission, purpose, and strategy among employees irrespective of geography, division, or function. For instance, policy changes delivered system-wide through video streaming concurrently to all sites reduces the risk of rumors getting out of hand.

- **E-training** translates into formal acquisition of skills development. Skills development can best be achieved through a formal training program. Such a program can be delivered in the classroom or online. Both classroom-based and online training have their place in an organization. Blending the two methods, choosing which method for which audience and which topics, is also plausible. Delivering training via electronic means saves time, reduces costs, and helps leverage the skills of specialized talent to larger numbers across the organization regardless of location.

Hindsight Is 20/20: Classroom Versus E-Learning

Is E-learning better (more effective) than classroom learning?

This is one of the most frequently asked questions.

For some topics and subject matter, the classroom might be the best medium. Most educational research that we're aware of concludes that retention is fairly limited after classroom learning. Is that the "high bar" for effectiveness in learning? Why do so many people like this method? Is it because of the human interaction that takes place? Or is it because it's familiar, comfortable, or makes one nostalgic? (Oops, this is supposed to be about answers, not more questions.)

Initial data from a variety of companies, such as KnowledgeNet, Inc., indicates that e-learning is equal to or more effective than traditional classroom learning. The best guesses as to why are centered around two characteristics: First, e-learning is available in modules measured in minutes, not hours or days so it is more easily digested. Second, e-learning is available 7×24, so the learners can access the content when they are in greatest need of it or most receptive to it. If a learner is more open and more receptive to the content, that learner will better retain it, regardless of the medium. Some call this the "teachable moment."

E-learning can be more flexible, accessible, and adaptable to each learner's needs, so the result is better retention. Does that mean it is more effective? Yes. It is even *more* effective if done well—with a match of appropriate subject matter and media choice— followed immediately by a short quiz, problem, or simulation.

- **E-assessment** translates into results. If assessment is not done, you are training for its own sake, not for the benefit of the individual or the organization. Why are you investing in training? What business results do you want to achieve with a knowledgeable and competent work force? Are you sure your work force has the knowledge and skills the company needs today? Who has the skills? What if the skill needs change as fast as the technology or the products and services change? How do you keep up? How do you gain confidence in the competence of the work force?

E-assessment, when complemented with a responsive e-training and e-communication program, offers a means to determine the efficacy of the knowledge-dissemination effort across an organization. Tools such as online or proctored exams, simulations, or scenario problems can be used to assess skills and knowledge. Electronic testing proves especially useful to deliver performance-simulation questions to candidates. These simulations more accurately reflect and predict skills, competence, and performance. The metrics generated through the assessment process are not only used to report on individual success, but they are also the basis for determining organizational success (for instance, the overall business impact of investing in an integrated system of communication, training, and assessment).

The Advantages from an Employee Perspective

From an employee perspective, an integrated approach to e-learning offers certain advantages as well:

- **E-communication** translates into increased awareness. Arguably, an organization is only as good as its front line, the employees who interact with customers. Employee success derives in part from clear, consistent, and successful communication throughout an organization. For example, the ability to download a sales presentation on product features and benefits the night before a presentation, or an hour before it, or even during a customer meeting, allows sales people to deliver more accurate (and perhaps current) information, and it gives the sales people confidence about their claims (especially if product features have been altered since the last presentation).

  Access to tools such as video on demand enables customer support personnel to view short clips demonstrating troubleshooting or installation tips on their workstations. The list of topics that are important to employees and that need to be consistent across the organization is endless: Organizational change, goals, products, priorities, consistent messages from executives to employees, and ethical-conduct reinforcement represent just a few of these topics. Effective and productive employees need to know about their job, the intentions of the company, the goals of the department, and perhaps even a particular customer—these are some of the reasons why e-communication is an essential success tool for every employee. It is why e-learning is a must for any organization that is geographically dispersed, regardless of the size of that organization.

- **E-training** translates into skills. The major advantage of e-learning is widespread access to training content. An advantage of e-learning from an employee perspective is that it extends the opportunity for mastery and for self-paced learning. Learners can repeat and practice certain tasks or factual information whenever necessary or desired (and according to their own schedule and availability). They can go back to the content as necessary for their job or for their customer. The kinds of training and content made available should reflect the needs of the intended audience and the outcome desired. This is usually best determined (and most appreciated) by the audience and management, not by a training organization (who are skilled professionals in their job, but not usually in sales or engineering or whatever they are building content for).

- **E-assessment** translates into career development. Employees value objective metrics that enable them to demonstrate improvement in their skills. Online exams, simulations, proctored exams, and certifications are valued by most employees as a measure for compensation or advancement decisions. Employees want to be confident in their competency, and they want a means to demonstrate it to the organization, not just their own manager. Consistent metrics in the organization's evaluation process means employees have broader visibility and greater chances for advancement, promotion, and recognition.

The pyramid metaphor offers a useful model for organizations to apply a comprehensive approach to learning, competence, and measurement. Anything short of a comprehensive approach will make real productivity advantages suspect. If productivity benefits are uncertain, or suspect, e-learning will remain, at best, an endeavor with questionable value and disappointing results, mired in endless *return-on-investment (ROI)* exercises.

Hindsight Is 20/20: What Is E-Learning (Really)?

It is more than just training; otherwise, it would have been named e-training. The term e-learning refers to using the web for information dissemination, communication, collaboration, assessment, and, oh yes, training.

E-learning is a broad category covering different ways of getting content (regardless of type or source) to learners when they need or want it. You are in the e-learning category when you deliver a course over the web; when you take a test online; when you participate in a virtual meeting using your PC; when you put technical documentation online for web deployment and use; and when you register for a classroom course using an online learning management system that tracks and reports on progress, results, and outcomes. You are using the tools and technologies of e-learning when you watch a live video from the CEO, HR, or the training group. Perhaps, you call up a video or audio on demand and catch up on the latest news from engineering, manufacturing, customer service, or the sales team. If so, you are participating in e-learning. Maybe, you create or capture content and make it available to others—structured training, formal messaging, or informal communications. If so, you are operating in the e-learning category.

It doesn't matter whether the "professionals" in the education and training industry call some content training, or education, or just information. That perspective is not the important one. It is the learners' perspective that counts, and to them it really doesn't matter what the training professionals call it. Learners call it necessary.

Learners wants easy and open access to whatever it is that is necessary to do their jobs better; to improve their chances for the next job or promotion; or to provide more customer satisfaction by being better informed, educated, and trained.

No Technology Religion

Distance learning, distance education, computer-based training, and instructional TV have all contributed to the body of knowledge around what is now refer to as e-learning. Technology limitations are a key factor that often impedes the adoption of electronically mediated learning. In certain cases, the technology is not ubiquitous (videoconferencing). In other cases, it is not interactive (instructional TV). And in other situations, it is not self-paced (satellite video). Even web-based learning that relies intensively on text-based content taxes the student to gather information that could more efficiently be gathered from an audio or video file. In the current age of voice, video, and data convergence, and Internet ubiquity over fast connections, Internet-based learning has gained in favor and popularity because of its possibilities and versatility.

If it is to work, managers must avoid the pitfall of letting the technology determine the nature of the program. Internet learning has a long way to go before it can be hailed as the perfect medium. In the training and development of soft skills, some organizations might determine that delivery of content over the web is not the right answer. Some have found that in areas where negotiation and sales skills are nurtured, more visual training approaches might be needed to ensure learning effectiveness. Technology must address the instructional needs of learners before it can fit a learning environment.

Hindsight Is 20/20: Out with the Old, in with the New

Should we eliminate all the classrooms and instructors we use today?

No, of course not. No one believes that, even those who ask it every time the topic comes up. Instructors and classrooms are wonderful ways to learn, communicate, and bond. However, they are not the best way in all cases for all people and all topics.

Consider this: Many people feared that movies would put live theater out of business. Years later, many people believed that the new invention called television would kill radio, live theater, and the movie industry. However, all those entertainment media choices coexist today and people choose among them, and books, and other choices. Did each new technology affect the existing entertainment choices? Yes, obviously, and each one evolved into the broad spectrum of entertainment choice we enjoy today.

Or look at it a different way: What is the best restaurant in your community? Not your favorite, but the local eatery that has the very best food in town. Do you eat there three times a day, every day? Probably not. Why? Is it too expensive? They don't serve breakfast? Service is too leisurely? So why not eat at a fast-food place three times a day, every day? It's convenient, not leisurely, and definitely not too expensive.

> The obvious and related point is that we have criteria that affects our choice of how we feed our bodies: how much time we have, how much we can afford, whether we need a full meal or just a piece of fruit, whether we are going to have a social meal or just fuel up to keep us going until a real meal at dinner. Again, it's about control, choice, and access to the appropriate mechanism that will meet your criteria for that moment.
>
> E-learning adds to the spectrum of choice for feeding your mind, your career, and your future. It is not about e-learning versus the classroom, it is about access and control over your choices of how to learn, when, and in what way. We should be able to choose how and what we are learning with the same ease that we choose where to have lunch. And that choice should take into account our preferences, our limitations of time and money, and our needs for different levels of detail depending on a number of factors.

Starting with the learning objectives and then choosing the best-suited delivery option often yields better results for learning programs. Cisco experience has demonstrated strong results using Internet learning, and, therefore, there is greater discussion on that topic. However, other companies may realize significant savings via satellite broadcasting. We obviously recommend that organizations focus on the *essential message* of productivity and just-in-time information, skills development, and skills assessment rather than on just e-training. The integrated approach to learning is still relevant regardless of the delivery medium.

A Premium on Skills

An especially germane factor in the business discussion is the economic premium assigned to high-level skills. In companies where employee interaction results in direct business benefits to the organization, such as consulting, sales, research, and professional services, productivity and increased skill levels generate clear advantages to employers. In other manufacturing and service sectors, the yields in productivity as a result of improved work-force performance, skills, and empowerment might not be as easily measured; however, they do exist.

A commitment to professional development needs to be made at the executive level. After that commitment of resources is made—whether based on performance metrics, ROI, value on investment, or management philosophy – pursuing the cherished goals of productivity through e-learning becomes more logical. Where companies are still struggling to define whether the human capital is indeed a strategic asset, a pursuit of productivity advantages will only be of marginal significance to executive management.

Learner Driven More Than Learner Centric

Volumes have been written about learner-centric curriculum development. Learner-centric content has always been positioned as superior to instructor-centered materials, and rightfully so, but harder to achieve in the traditional classroom. An integrated approach to e-learning aims at making available learner-driven tools.

Learner driven goes beyond learner centric in that it essentially places the control of the event in the hands of the learner. What is left for the organization to do is create incentives, set objectives, and offer the environment for the learner to take advantage of e-learning.

Empirical evidence suggests that many organizations focus on logging training hours completed by an employee. When training departments are dedicated to micromanaging the learning activity rather than the objectives and the environment, the learning process can hardly be termed learner driven. Organizations in that pattern are measuring the wrong thing (hours), so success will prove less meaningful to the company than to the training department.

Target Audiences

A wide variety of business sectors currently utilize e-learning, as shown in the following list. This list identifies the different business sectors and then states the percentage of companies within a particular sector that are now engaged in e-learning within their organizations:

- Banking/financial services/insurance: 65%
- Government: 43%
- Pharmaceuticals: 37%
- Health care: 35%
- Information technology/high tech: 35%
- Communications: 29%
- Manufacturing: 29%
- Utilities: 22%
- Retail: 17%
- Transportation: 15%
- Education: 11%
- Other: 12%[1]

The e-learning approach described in this book aims at generating a global view of learning and development within an organization. Instead of focusing on the training department versus the IT department versus the marketing communications group, building an integrated approach to e-learning calls for establishing a cohesive effort to empower the employee, an effort that will certainly require cross-function collaboration.

Measuring the value or ROI should not be difficult after the key benefits of e-learning have been identified: for example, speed to market, time to competence, improved customer service, and strategic advantages. Another strong business benefit is the impact of a cohesive learning system on customer satisfaction. Knowing which metric or benefit to measure to assess the value of e-learning is critical to the evaluation process.

End Notes

[1] Source: brandon-hall.com

CHAPTER 3

E-LEARNING UNDER THE MICROSCOPE

> ### *Key Take-Away*
> Internet learning has offered Cisco quantifiable productivity benefits worth $142 million in one study and a return of $16 for every dollar spent on a particular e-learning program.

An organization owes its employees and, in many cases, its resellers and customers, a compelling vision, quality instruction and performance management, and just and reasonable compensation. The productivity advantages of e-learning result from multiplying the effectiveness of the message. Internet learning, or e-learning, is a delivery process built around the notion that, other things being equal, a connected work force is more informed, motivated, and coordinated as a team. The e-learning process encompasses a host of components that stimulate work-force development; these are discussed in this chapter.

A thorough learning process, however, is never a substitute for poor or unresponsive learning content. *Subject-matter experts (SMEs)* who can offer valuable content and information to make workers more productive will always remain in demand. The effectiveness of how well that content is communicated over an e-learning medium depends, however, on a robust process.

Benefits of Formulating a Business Case

Business leaders everywhere are faced with certain common objectives, such as the following:

- How do I increase revenue?
- How do I strengthen customer loyalty and retention?
- How do I reduce time to competency? How do I increase organizational agility?
- How do I increase the efficiency and effectiveness of current operations?
- How do I differentiate from my competitors?

In their efforts to achieve these business objectives, decision makers in organizations rely on communications tools to execute their strategies. Internet learning serves as a tool to improve productivity by strengthening an organization's ability to execute. E-learning offers organizations the productivity advantage by not just improving training, but also communication and accountability within an organization. So how can a learning effort have such a far-reaching impact within the organization?

Chapter 3: E-Learning Under the Microscope

Hindsight Is 20/20: How Real Is It?

Is e-learning just hype about networking capabilities, like the dot.com bubble was? Is e-learning another training experiment that is just going to fail or be inconsequential?

Two things that have plagued the training/education industry for decades are an absence of accountability to the business it serves and a lack of credibility with the various audiences.

Accountability is being addressed by levels of assessment, certification, and management reporting about metrics important to the business (for example, how customer satisfaction is impacted by better-informed and better-educated sales or support people) that was not really possible without web-based tools such as assessments.

This accountability has several new aspects. We can track and report on progress, test results, and usage to hold learners accountable for what they are supposed to know to do their jobs well. It gives managers and decision makers confidence in the competence of our work force. More importantly, decision makers can roll that information up organizationally and analyze the knowledge and skill factors at a macro level.

In addition, we can hold content creators/authors accountable for the accuracy and "freshness" of the materials they create, and we can survey and analyze data to determine whether we are using the proper medium for different types of content. Accountability is what separates this new capability of e-learning from the previous incarnations of classrooms, laser discs, multimedia CD-ROMs, videotapes, and so on.

As for audience credibility, when we use consistent tools and processes, we can decentralize the creation of content to the SMEs around the company. The SMEs can be salespeople, engineers, product marketing staff, executives, or whoever is the best at his job and is willing to share what he knows (so that, hopefully, others can replicate or adapt that information to their job). When the best salesperson in an organization speaks about selling, the rest of the sales team listens (if only to berate the comments later).

No one has greater credibility in an audience than someone who has been there, done that, and has a reputation for doing it better than everyone else in the room, or online, or wherever. We trainers seldom have those credentials or support.

Chapter 2, "Internet Learning — A Productivity Tool," discussed e-learning as a productivity tool with three components as key factors leading to successful deployment of e-learning or Internet learning in an organization: e-communication, e-training, and e-assessment. E-communication refers to the information, communication, collaboration, and knowledge sharing that takes place in an organization. E-training, on the other hand, refers to training delivered through electronic media. Finally, e-assessment refers to the evaluation (through exams, tests, quizzes, and certifications) of content understanding and retention. The following sections review each of the three components in more detail.

E-Communication

Organizations often refer to e-communication as *knowledge sharing*. Many decision makers consider e-communication to be the same as e-learning. For the purpose of analysis, identifying e-communication and e-training as distinct components of e-learning offers greater insight into each application and more clarity about deployment methods, design, and intent.

In a pyramid metaphor, e-communication constitutes the foundational (bottom-most) layer. Many organizations already have in place the underlying IT infrastructure required to enable e-communication and e-training. At Cisco, over the years, e-communication has presented itself as a strong offshoot of the learning infrastructure. As a result, not only has e-communication in most cases taken precedence over e-training, but also the impact of e-communication has been broader in terms of employees, channel partners, and customers reached. (See Figure 3-1.)

Figure 3-1 *Deployment Methods*

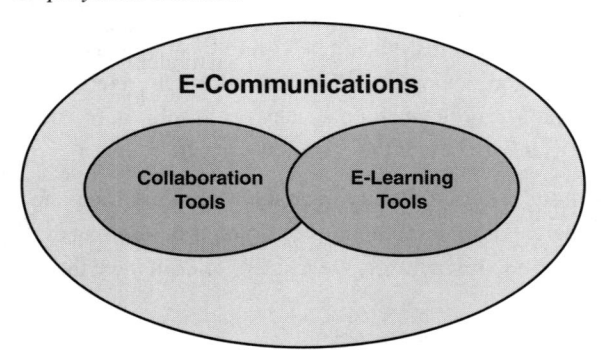

From a business perspective, the following list identifies just some of the specific benefits of e-communication:

- **Time to market**—Enables product managers to communicate features and benefits of new products and services to a large audience of sales force and channel partners
- **Organizational agility and morale**—Offers more frequent and consistent executive messaging about business status, goals, or new policies
- **Customer focus**—Shares customer feedback and solutions more rapidly with the customer service or support network
- **Customer intimacy**—Provides customers with access to executives and experts within the company
- **Sales force readiness**—Offers anytime-anyplace access to the latest and most accurate product and service information for those "feet on the street"
- **Reduced cost of access**—Reduces cost of communications in terms of travel, telecommunications, event management, and time away from work

Widespread adoption of information technologies means that organizations now have more communication tools at their disposal. The use of these newer tools, including e-communication, has produced significant work-place integration and work-force advantages.

Beyond Awareness: Retention and Motivation

To communicate with internal audiences, organizational leaders have long relied on tools such as voicemail broadcasts, e-mail alerts, announcements on the corporate intranet, and articles in organizational e-newsletters. Web portals enable audience participants, at their convenience, to access updated organizational information. These tools work well to convey awareness-level information, but organizations still must confirm audience understanding and adoption of the content conveyed via these tools. Comprehension is the key factor bearing on retention of a message.

Perhaps the messaging goals of an organization extend beyond awareness to motivation or retention. If so, IP video offers significant advantages over other tools. IP video enables trainers to both explain and demonstrate a concept simultaneously, which enhances clarity and viewer understanding. In addition, people tend to find visual media (such as IP video) more personal, a fact that may influence viewers to internalize messages conveyed via IP video. If the video broadcast occurs in real time (synchronous), the broadcast may even create a "congregation" effect that boosts target-audience participation.

Besides video, online and multimedia tools such as simulations and games offer the audience a more comprehensive understanding of technologies, tools, and terminologies. At Cisco, employee and customer audiences have responded favorably to the use of simulations and games for knowledge sharing (of both concepts and technologies).

Hindsight Is 20/20: Shortcuts Do Not Really Pay Back the Investment

Some organizations may be asking what seems like a simple question: How do we get our content online? However, this question isn't as simple as it first appears. This approach represents, at best, a patch (and, at worst, a waste of resources). Merely digitizing material developed for the classroom and making in available online usually results in suboptimal content and low satisfaction levels among learners. If an organization has no other way to present the material, this is a viable option. It is also a viable option for those organizations that consider this a first step, one that moves the audience toward the web. However, organizations should not be lulled into reliance on this shortcut. Remember: Classroom materials need instructors!

Converting text to HTML and placing that text online is relatively simple and will make that content available to large numbers of people quickly and consistently. Do not put a lot of resources into this effort, however, especially internal resources. Contract this out to specialists, perhaps vendors with automated tools, and be ready to throw it away after four to nine months of use. It will be received with minimum resistance at first because of the ease of access the learner enjoys. However, when that access is taken for granted, when it is woven into the fabric of the job, the cry will go out for higher-quality content, new media types, and more engaging delivery.

That's when you know the grace period is over, that e-learning is going to be important to your organization, and that your real challenge has finally begun.

Video over IP: An E-Communication Breakthrough

Adoption of video has been the hallmark of e-communication/e-training efforts and has generated a substantial portion of the $142 million in productivity gains for Cisco in fiscal year 2003. (See Table 3-1.) Through effective use of video, Cisco has reduced the geographic barriers among its managers, its employees, channel partners, and customers. Finally, instead of the student going to knowledge, knowledge was coming to the student in all three dimensions: voice, video, and data.

Table 3-1 Fiscal Year 2002 Cisco E-Learning Benefits

Internet Business Solutions	Cost Avoidance	Time Efficiencies	Internet Capabilities Benefit
Web Based Training	$16M	$53M	$69M
Cisco TV	$18M	$1M	$19M
Video-on Demand	$2M	$4M	$6M
Virtual Classroom	$5M	$2M	$7M
Lab Simulations	$32M	$9M	$41M
Total			$142M

Source: Cisco IBSG, Internet Capabilities Analysis, FY 2003

Whether in the form of live broadcasts or on-demand streaming media, the use of video over IP has enhanced the quality and reduced the cost of executive communications, product introductions, competitive analysis, and market updates. These video solutions provide clear, consistent, and accessible communications. By reducing layers of messages, video use results in consistent communication across the organization. The nonverbal cues of the speaker (tone, tenor, eye movement, facial expressions, and so on) enhance the intimacy with the audience, eventually improving retention of the message.

When using video as a means of communications and delivery, organizations have two options:

- **Broadcast video**—Broadcast video over IP allows real-time (synchronous) live presentations. The participant can watch, ask questions via instant messaging, and see the presentations and any additional screenshots or graphics.

- **Video on demand**—Video on demand, on the other hand, offers anytime-anyplace (asynchronous) access to the video, audio, and accompanying slide presentation. The content for video on demand can be anything, including the following:
  - *Past broadcasts or those created on demand*—VoD can include past broadcast (synchronous) video presentations or those video presentations created solely on demand (asynchronous).
  - *Knowledge bytes*—Sales and sales-support personnel may receive an e-mail alert with a short (30-second to 5-minute) video that demonstrates a specific solution, appropriate use of a specific feature, or troubleshooting of a technical problem.
  - *Message and training*—Longer-duration VoD training modules. A series of modules complete a lesson or a meeting. Each module is about 10 to 20 minutes in length.

As a medium, video has constraints, not the least of which is the audience attention span. The attention span of a participant reviewing a video presentation, for example, begins to taper after 5 to 7 minutes and becomes nonexistent soon after 15 minutes.[1] Some speakers who excel in face-to-face communication struggle in the two-dimensional realm of video presentations, which does not have live feedback.

Bandwidth considerations, especially at the individual level, remain an important consideration. Many viewers, especially in areas where broadband is not fully deployed, still use dial-up modems to access content over the Internet. Such individuals might be hard to reach with a video message only unless a downloadable version of the message is available or the message is available in an alternative audio-only format.

Besides access, factors such as security of the information, crisp quality, and uninterrupted stream of video affect content acceptance. A weak delivery effort is likely to distract—and worse still, discourage—the learner.

The strength of the visual media is hard to dispute. As the adoption of broadband grows, organizational networks assume greater capability to carry IP video, and decision makers become more willing to communicate using video as a tool, the increased role of video as a means of knowledge sharing within organizations will be inevitable.

E-Training

In 2000, Cisco needed recertification on International Organization for Standardization, commonly referred to as ISO 9001. The task meant preparing several thousand individuals in customer service, manufacturing, and engineering departments on ISO 9001 guidelines. Based on the events three years prior, the ISO readiness training program had budgeted $1.4 million in travel, classroom, content development, and materials expenses over a period of four months.

Transforming the ISO recertification training program to an Internet learning platform took a little more than three weeks. Voice, video, and data presentations were prepared along with accompanying tests. The program was delivered over the web. Not only did Cisco pass its inspections, but it also was rated second nationwide in ISO readiness that year. Compared to the $1.4 million of three years ago, the training program ended up costing Cisco less than $17,000 because of e-learning.

With such applications, Cisco has taken advantage of Internet learning in different content areas to reduce costs and time to market. Following is a brief review of the e-training evolution at Cisco:[2]

1. Evolution of e-training

   E-training at Cisco has moved from a content-centric approach to a learner-centric approach, as shown in Figure 3-2 and the following list.

Figure 3-2   *The Cisco Vision for E-Learning*

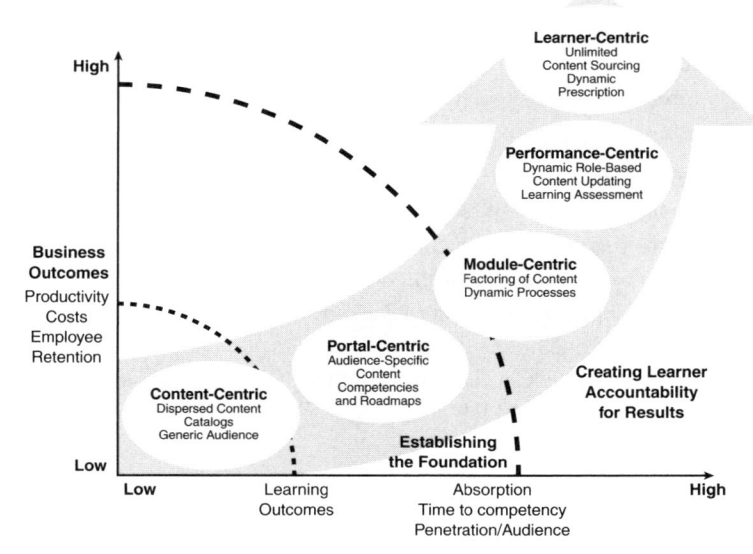

a **Content centric**—Cisco initiated e-training with a content focus. Each product group, functional group, and corporate function developed its own web-based training site. The result was an array of dispersed and disparate learning systems and catalogs for audiences to search through for content. Employees could not find the information they needed unless they knew which catalog or website to search.[3]

b **Portal centric**—The information was aggregated based on communities with common needs and interests. The creation of the *Field E-Learning Connection (FELC)* framework was a success under this model; other portals for partners, manufacturing, and leadership development were also created. The success of portals came from the ease of access for users when searching, retrieving, and leveraging content on a specific topic. For the first time, learning was at the learners' fingertips.

c **Module centric**—The innovation in content development occurred with the implementation of *reusable learning objects (RLOs)* and *reusable information objects (RIOs)*. Initiated in 1997, objects began to have a noticeable impact at Cisco in 1999. By definition, RLO or RIO involve creating, tagging, and storing content in small chunks of content to allow ease of searching, retrieving, presenting, and repurposing. Utilizing a corporate-supported IT platform for tagging the content, Cisco developers captured, organized, blended, reused, and shared learning and information objects more readily in their courses. The success in the training area fostered a large-scale meta-data framework project extending this principle to broader context areas of marketing, technical documents, customer services, and employee updates.

d **Performance centric**—The next stage of e-training enabled managers to tie job requirements, training history, and development plans together with performance appraisals to systemically manage their work force. Nurturing the intellectual capital and developing their employees became easier for managers as they gained better access to documented and reportable results on their team's learning achievements. Coordination with the system was initiated during this phase of the evolution.

Chapter 3: E-Learning Under the Microscope

e **Learner centric**—Learner-centric training involved creating personalized content based on the performance and learning profile of the user. Dynamically displayed through a My Learning or My Development (see chapter 7, "Targeted Learning: Are You *Indeed* Ready?") page, learners were able to review their strengths and weaknesses to adopt a customized learning plan accordingly with input from their manager.

2 A productivity portal: FELC

In 1998, the size of the Cisco sales force was 5000 and was projected to more than double over the following 18 to 24 months. The challenge of keeping a sales force trained and current on hundreds of complex products that evolved every six to nine months remained a daunting task. At Cisco, newly hired sales personnel traveled to corporate or regional training sites for several five-day courses each year, courses that delivered training for one product line to the entire field in a classroom setting. This required up to 200 training sessions for each course to reach everyone worldwide.

The demand for sales readiness created the first portal at Cisco for e-training. It was also used extensively for e-communication, providing 80 percent of all the technical and product information that Cisco salespeople needed to know at a single place on the web. The portal included content such as the following:

- A VoD menu that searches disparate databases and systems at Cisco to find modules that are relevant to a learner's interest or need

- Online lab programs sessions that enable learners to connect to a hands-on, remote lab and receive instructional directions upon their arrival

- Robust reporting capabilities that enable sales managers to track and monitor their employees' curriculum, understand exactly which of their employees have taken and passed the assessment tests, and assess employee baseline product knowledge and progress

- Electronic access to Cisco experts or "e-mentors," who can respond via e-mail, phone, or virtually meet learners in a lab (and connect to their screen and walk them through an exercise)

- Registration system and a web catalog of classroom and online leader-led sessions offered across the globe, as well as searchable documents and presentations
- Online tests to complement learning as an aid for identifying knowledge and skills gaps

The sales readiness process became more efficient, timelier, and more relevant to a constantly changing environment. By using the FELC, the Cisco field sales organization could do the following:

- Access the latest information on new Cisco products and evolving technologies
- Spend more time on the job and less on training-related travel (which reduced field-training costs by 40 percent to 60 percent)
- Spend more quality "face time" with customers (in fact, 40 percent more)

To incorporate accountability as a part of the Cisco learning process, Cisco developed management reports that track participation, progress, and completion, as well as assessment scores and certification attainment.

3 Five steps to content development

So how does content development take place in an e-learning environment for training purposes? Cisco has adopted a five-step approach to content development that allows the organization to leverage content readily across multiple delivery media and repurpose it to accommodate content modification.

The e-training development model (see Figure 3-3) unfolds in a complementary relationship with content sources, such as SMEs. The SME may be anyone inside or outside the organization who serves as a knowledge broker, including a corporate training specialist, product manager, human resource representative, or a salesperson. The development model scales to support the business drivers at each stage of

Chapter 3: E-Learning Under the Microscope

any content area's natural evolution. The more detailed model used for the more mature content serves as a baseline and goal for all early-development cycles.

Figure 3-3   *Cisco E-Learning Process Model*

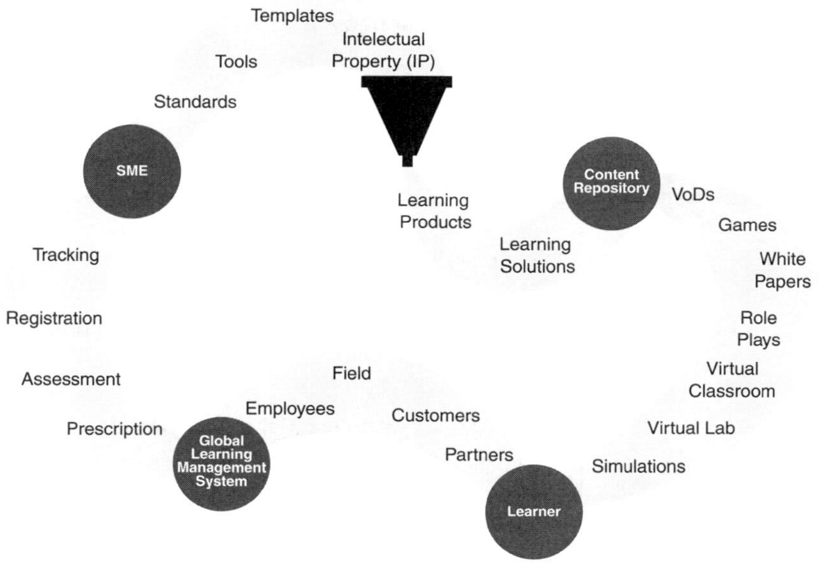

One of the key features of the five steps is the reuse of content (RIOs and RLOs). Essentially, a classic technique for reducing the cost of e-learning development, RIO/RLO refers to creating e-learning content in small chunks (chapters, modules) so that it may be reused or edited (perhaps even deleted) without having to incur a large cost during revisions. The five steps for content development are as follows:

Step 1. Analyze learning. In this step, the organization collects learner-, industry-, and skill-specific data. Inferences are drawn and summarized from the data in preparation to design the training.

Step 2. Review the findings from Step 1, incorporating standards, tools, and templates into a learning design. This review must focus on structural, treatment, and deployment methods required to balance learner needs and business drivers in an appropriate fashion.

Step 3. Develop content using the applicable processes and associated workflow standards based on the final design and deployment strategies. The training materials, including relevant design data, are marked using a standard meta-tag vocabulary and stored in a repository (intellectual property). Content development that includes RIOs/RLOs enables organizations to repurpose the content for courseware development, maintenance, and updates.

To develop learning products, blend the most appropriate pieces of content from the database repository with the delivery vehicle of choice to achieve the different learning objectives and reach different audiences.

Step 4. Deliver the content through various mechanisms based on learning objectives and audience needs. After a course has been assembled, it may be delivered via e-training or synchronous instruction with modest alterations.

Step 5. Run an administrative system parallel to the content-development process to manage, track, assess, and prescribe customized content for any given learner. The process generates feedback using the assessment and accountability tools for improvement in development and delivery processes.

Specific development or productivity advantages derived from this model include the following:

- Reduced redevelopment of related or redundant training content
- Reduced number of SME interviews, returning key technical resources to higher-value job roles
- Reduced number of resources focused on routine development tasks, allowing for greater focus on scaling key tasks or resources
- Reduced redevelopment based on misleading feedback
- Increased speed of development or time to market

E-training at Cisco is closely tied to assessment. The proof of learning is in performance. And performing on tests, exams, quizzes, and certifications is an indicator of learning. The demand for e-training is fueled by assessments, which are in turn fueled by performance evaluation and/or incentives.

> ### *Hindsight Is 20/20: What About Production Values*
>
> "I've done self-paced stuff before, and watched some VHS video courses … is it just me or is most of this stuff boring? Some of it is just plain bad!"
>
> Sadly, this is true. A lot of content out there is bad for you. Which means it is not conducive to learning. It's not all bad, and what's bad for you may not be for someone else. (However, I do believe that there is a universal "bad," and it's not all that rare.) The problem is that this industry is actually only five to seven years old. Technology is the driver of this new industry we call e-learning, that and need to make a profit to survive the path taken by previous dot.coms.
>
> We are where the movie industry was 100 years ago. When moving pictures were first invented, the camera was placed in a stationary location, and someone filmed a theatrical play or dancers coming to or across the camera's field of view. These were wonderful things for people who could not see a play or dancers, but they were usually bad movies.
>
> Today, whether text online, video on demand, audio and slides, or whatever, we are making a large number of "bad movies." The proof is in the frequency of the awful question "How do we get our courses on line?" The flaw in this approach is that, if executed, content designed to be led by a facilitator or instructor is now a self-paced lesson. It is the worst of both worlds: content repurposed for a different medium; and no skillful, knowledgeable instructor to save the day via interpretation and experience.
>
> Self-paced, self-started, or whatever you want to call it does not have to be structured, formal, or boring. It is best received when short, informal, and focused on the audience requirement rather than the speaker/writer agenda.

E-Assessment

Assessment refers to exams, online tests, and certifications that help determine whether someone has acquired the desired knowledge and skills. Even online quizzes can serve as a means of assessing learner retention and understanding of content. Planners should ensure that some form of assessment forms a core component of a learning effort.

Cisco experience has shown tremendous success with certifications. (See Figure 3-4.) Any discussion about Cisco certifications would be incomplete without explaining the *Cisco Certified Internetwork Expert (CCIE)* phenomenon at Cisco. CCIE is the Cisco premier networking certification to date. The industry, time and again, has referred to it as one of the most robust networking certification available in the information technology sector. CCIE credibility results from its performance-based testing. Currently, fewer than 10,000 individuals worldwide hold the CCIE certification, making them an elite group of top networking talent.

Figure 3-4 *Certification Statistics*

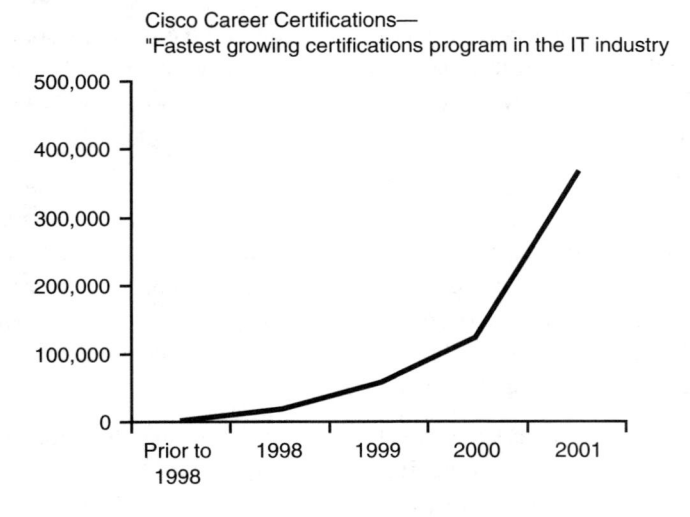

Cisco Career Certifications—
"Fastest growing certifications program in the IT industry

The exam model developed and implemented under the CCIE program has served as a model for others in the technical industry. Besides sitting through a qualifying exam, a candidate has to pass a full-day grueling lab by demonstrating hands-on skills with setting up a network. The nature of tasks presented has made passing the lab exam on the first attempt a cherished goal for some of the most astute networking professionals.

Chapter 3: E-Learning Under the Microscope

So what drives organizations and their employees to pursue certifications? Organizations seek certain business advantages from certifications, whereas employees expect to strengthen their career prospects by pursuing certifications.

1   Benefits to employers

CCIE performance expectations are well established around the world. When an IP network goes down, many customers expect that a CCIE will be able to bring it back up. With the extent of goodwill and reputation that the CCIE program has generated, networking talent with CCIE certification remains in short supply.

From an employer's perspective, certifications serve as a means of validating technical expertise, improving profitability, and retaining talent. The need for candidates to be aligned with the business drivers for the organization cannot be overemphasized. Key benefits of certifications for employers include the following:

a   Certification constitutes a tool for assessing employees.

In an environment of resource optimization, employers are more sensitive to performance benchmarks. Maintaining and upgrading certifications is a way for a professional to establish technical prowess. More firms are now adopting certifications as part of the job specifications for certain positions. In an era of consolidation and restructuring, an IT professional could well be reporting to new leadership, even on the same job. Certifications help to identify certified individuals within an organization as proactive employees who are eager to learn and increase their value to an organization.[5]

b   Certification helps achieve productivity objectives.

Survey data and anecdotal evidence suggests that networking credentials create a better understanding of solutions and deployment practices among certified individuals. In a market where productivity and profits are critical, the value of ensuring that a technical team can bring a networking project under time and budget cannot be overstated. Certified professionals provide employers confidence in their networking caliber. At the very least, certified individuals demonstrate a strong grasp of fundamentals and a willingness to learn advanced concepts.[6]

    c Slow markets are dynamic, too.

Although growth in the IT sector slowed from 2001 to 2003 relative to previous years, the pace of change has not abated. Changing customer needs are constantly reshaping the industry with demands for new solutions and services. Moreover, growth in emerging technology segments, such as security, IP telephony, and content networking, has generated demand for new skills in the networking industry. Employers seeking to respond to the changing marketplace find certifications a valuable resource for verifiable skills development. Certifications enable employers to keep their essential resource—people and technical expertise—versatile when responding to networking demands and ensuring consistent quality in production networks.[7]

2 Benefits to candidates

    a Certifications enhance job mobility.

In times of changing markets and evolving needs, certifications enable individuals to enter and pursue areas with the highest growth potential. A networking team that was once committed to infrastructure expansion can be redirected through appropriate training and certifications to deploy new applications, solutions, and services on the existing infrastructure. Upgrading skills in step with networking trends ensures that networking professionals remain versatile in offering value to the organization. In a slow market, this is one way for team members to ensure that they remain relevant and indispensable to the organization.[10]

    b Certifications increase job security.

Directly related to versatility is job security. Knowledge workers who can offer a wider array of skills to the employer are less likely to be adversely affected when teams are restructured. Many companies rely on certified employees to successfully obtain consulting projects and contract awards. Eliminating the very asset that constitutes a firm's competitive advantage is highly unlikely in any organization, and even less so in service and consulting firms.[8]

c Certifications improve compensation.

   Certified employees who demonstrate critical skills are prime candidates for the scarce performance raises that organizations offer in difficult economic times. The relevance of training and certification to the employer's line of business and the level of competency achieved are key factors that influence the level of an employee's reward.[9]

Although we have discussed the Cisco experience in assessment by reviewing certifications as a means of assessment, many industries may find that internal quizzes, online tests, or proctored exams might serve the purpose of determining who has the requisite skills. On a more day-to-day level, supervisors might be able to make decisions about the strengths and weaknesses of employees based on their job performance. The essence of assessment is to assume a formal and objective process for determining whether employees indeed possess the desired skills.

Determining a Value on Investment for E-Learning

Whether it's a nonprofit or for-profit business, financial metrics will generate a healthy and meaningful debate focused on quantifying the actual advantages of an e-learning initiative. A study concluded in April 2004 at Cisco shows that for every dollar Cisco spent on one specific e-learning initiative in fiscal year 2003, the company received $16 in value. Yes, the value was 16 times the expenditure.

The e-learning initiative for the study was *Partner E-Learning Connection (PEC)*, a Cisco portal dedicated to delivering learning content to resellers without fee. The study was based on an annual reseller survey to identify the use of e-learning and how that use affects business. When this study was conducted, the PEC was in its fourth year of operation and was cited by resellers as a significant factor in increased sales.

Arriving at the Numbers

The analysis for arriving at the 1:16× ratio discussed in the preceding section is based on the reseller survey conducted by Walker Information in July 2003 on the effectiveness of the PEC e-learning portal. The respondents for the survey included the employees working within Cisco reseller organizations. Presented here are the findings from the survey:

   a Ninety-five percent of the respondents reported that PEC e-learning program made them more productive in selling, supporting, and servicing Cisco products.

   b On average, respondents reported saving nine and a half hours per month per person in selling, supporting, and servicing Cisco products as a result of the PEC program.

   c Eighty two percent of the respondents reported increased sales as a result of the PEC program.

   d On average, respondents reported increased sales of $9700 per month as a result of the PEC program.

Following are the findings:

- **Finding 1 (based on a, b, c, and d)**—In total, estimated partner increases in sales are more than $1.2 billion per year as a result of PEC. (Equation: 13,000 users per month * $9700/month/person * 12 months. * 82% = $1.2B/year.)

- **Finding 2**—Cisco avoided costs of a little over $40 million in fiscal year 2003 by using the PEC program in lieu of instructor-led training by the Cisco sales force, roadshows, labs, and other methods that would have been required to deliver similar amounts of training if PEC did not exist.

After adjusting for reseller margins, development costs—depreciation, and overheads—the study concludes the following:

For every dollar Cisco spent on PEC in fiscal year 2003, the company received $16 in value (that is, costs avoided plus profits on incremental sales reported by resellers minus expenses to operate and provide content for PEC).

Principles Behind the Numbers

So what did Cisco learn from the PEC experience! What was it that led this e-learning program to achieve this attention-getting financial performance? Here are just four of the practices:

- E-learning as a conscious investment.

    Financial projections, user feedback, and evidence of productivity gains in the reseller channel were key indicators of success in the beginning. Based on the success in those early months, senior management in three different organizations made a conscious decision to increase investment in this e-learning initiative.

- Beyond training, e-learning covers assessment and communication.

    E-learning was found to be more productive at Cisco when offered to learners as a package of e-assessment, e-training, and e-communication components. Training is only one aspect of e-learning at Cisco. E-assessment and e-communication complete the capability. Assessments, through online tests and certifications, drive learners to content by instilling accountability in the learning process. E-communication tools that support collaboration, communication, and information and knowledge sharing on a day-to-day basis enable individuals to weave learning into the fabric of their day.

- E-learning aligns with the sales process.

    E-learning efforts at Cisco have gained immense acceptance internally by aligning with the sales process—both internal and partner. If the sales force or the sales channel ends up being more productive through the use of e-learning, the recurring metric of increased revenue is always on hand to show the value of the project, and a host of advocates are readily available to offer testimonials.

    Some training managers express frustration with cost-saving numbers from e-learning because they believe those metrics are a one-time phenomenon. They believe that a financial benefit that was recurring each year would be a more valuable metric in making a case for continued support of e-learning within an organization. What better metric than product revenue? It's annual, starts from zero each year, and gets the attention of the decision makers immediately and often.

- E-learning offers economies of scale.

    When the technology infrastructure and content expertise are in place, e-learning makes the incremental cost of reaching new learners remarkably lower. By exploiting the classic technology advantage—economies of scale—offerings are extended using e-learning to a larger base of learners. For organizations such as Cisco, with a large number of reseller partners and their employees benefiting from e-learning, the overall productivity impact multiplies even more.

Hindsight Is 20/20: Dollars and Sense

How much money can I save doing this?

You can save an extraordinary amount of travel-related dollars, as well as those costs associated with facilities, instructors, and some of the printing costs (but not all, because some people want hard-copy books or guides even in a live or self-paced e-learning situation).

We estimate that in the United States, you save $2400 per week per student if students choose e-learning over the classroom (in travel expenses, facilities, and instructor time only). Classroom hardware and software vary too dramatically to include them in the costs and variables estimate.

The downside of this savings is that it is actually only noticeable for the first year. In each subsequent year, those expense dollars will not be budgeted and therefore cannot be "saved." For this reason, it is important to have baseline data about how many students traveled to class last year and the year before that, so you can demonstrate savings based on reduced attendance. It's a possible source of funding if you choose to document that "the company used to spend $8 million annually on travel for training. This year we only spent $5 million. Can you move some of those savings to the learning budget? $5 million? $7 million? How about $2 million?"

You can also save some money on development and deployment.

Conclusion

A sound e-learning business plan with financial metrics should also be backed by a commitment to make it happen. Will that turn a training group into a small profit center with unusual partners throughout the organization? Might that change the training manager's job from one that focuses on learning to one that focuses on the business of learning? Might that get the training organization to begin viewing content as "product" and learners as "markets"? The answers to all these questions are "maybe." No one ever said that change agents are insulated from the change they cause.

Endnotes

[1] Galagan, Patricia. "Delta Force," *Training* Magazine, Lakewood Publications, May 2002

[2] Kelly, Tom and Diane Bauer. "Managing Intellectual Capital at Cisco," *Handbook of Knowledge Management*, Volume 2, Edited by C. W. Holsapple, Springer-Verlag, December 2002

[3] ibid

[4] ibid

[5] Nanjiani, Nader. "Identifying Talent in Turbulent Times," *Certifications* Magazine, MediaTec Publishing, May 2002

[5] ibid

[6] ibid

[7] ibid

[8] ibid

[9] ibid

CHAPTER 4

BearingPoint Makes a Grand Slam with Internet Learning: A Case Study

The Business Case for E-Learning

> ### *Key Take-Away*
>
> Instead of viewing their function as training and viewing themselves as trainers, today's training managers should view learning as a business transformation opportunity and view themselves as change agents.
>
> —Learning and Development, BearingPoint

In a business where intellect is capital and knowledge is an asset, faster learning means increased speed to market with solutions and services. BearingPoint shows how Internet learning convinced, almost overnight, the consulting organization and its consultants to adopt e-business practices for their company and their clients.

Case Summary

The BearingPoint case study highlights how a learning and development organization committed to meeting business imperatives generated top-line and bottom-line advantages for the organization. The business imperatives drove the need for speed, which in turn yielded greater flexibility, professional development, and improved access to knowledge for employees. The company benefited from the lower cost of delivery, greater return on work-force development, reduced time to market with talent, and consistent quality in consulting practices. All this was accomplished through meager upfront investments and a lean learning and development organization.

Chapter 4: BearingPoint Makes a Grand Slam with Internet Learning

Introduction

An E-Learning Expo and Conference 2001 survey found that two thirds of all companies rated their current e-learning initiatives as unsuccessful at affecting behavioral change. The most common reasons cited for not affecting change were lack of interaction, lack of engaging content, and content not addressing business needs.

With the mixed results on Internet learning being reported in industry sources, a skeptic may wonder whether investment in Internet learning indeed yields results for organizations other than Cisco. The answer is an unequivocal yes from one of the most respected consulting groups in the world, BearingPoint. The consulting company demonstrated Internet learning success based on a model that incorporates effective use of the pyramid metaphor: e-training, e-communication, and e-assessment.

The Point of Inflexion

The moment of change arrived at BearingPoint in 1999, when the company committed to making all employees savvy in the ways of e-business. Up to that point, the organization had only known traditional (face-to-face) learning. The company's learning and development organization, had 90 days to develop a training solution and another 90 days to deliver it. The task was clear: Over a 6-month period, the group had to ensure that each employee in the work force of thousands had acquired a fundamental understanding of e-business practices.

As the team scrambled for a solution in the summer of 1999, the Internet presented itself as the most viable means of reaching a work force as busy as that of BearingPoint. The Learning and Development team at BearingPoint realized that traditional face-to-face delivery would leave them shy of their objectives. With almost 60 percent of the work force traveling at any given point in time, the last thing the employees needed was more time away from home at a training course. More importantly, taking time away from client commitments and the corresponding opportunity cost of lost consulting revenue would make the project cost-prohibitive.

The challenge was a point of inflexion in the training and development timeline for the organization. Present in front of them was an opportunity to break away from the practices of the past. As a team, the learning and development organization turned to the Internet as a means of transforming the learning environment at BearingPoint—and it has not looked back since.

With the delivery mode determined, the group relied on DigitalThink (now Convergys E-Learning Solutions), a custom e-learning company, to host and monitor the adoption of the e-business course among BearingPoint employees. Convergys also provided the company support with course authoring and packaging. The team formulated the learning objectives and gathered credible subject matter experts and sources for the content to support those objectives. White papers, briefs, CD-ROMs, and PowerPoint presentations complemented the course.

Six months later, the team had successfully developed and delivered the course as an anytime-anyplace learning effort. The objective had been met. Because it was tied to bonus eligibility, the course had a 95 percent completion rate. An exam was tied to the course to assess understanding and knowledge acquired through the learning process. On a scale of 5, the satisfaction rating for the course was a 4.2. In its first initiative, BearingPoint had leveraged e-communication, e-assessment, and e-training to achieve the learning goal.

Chapter 4: BearingPoint Makes a Grand Slam with Internet Learning

Building on Success

The profitability potential of Internet learning was hardly lost on the planners at BearingPoint. From that first success, the team at BearingPoint understood that by increasing the deployment of Internet learning, BearingPoint could not only minimize the cost and opportunity cost of travel, but it could also increase revenue. In the world of consulting, where profitability matters, keeping consultants billable and realizing a higher rate for their billable hours ensures revenue growth. By cultivating specialty skills among its promising consultants through a short turnaround e-training project, BearingPoint stood to improve the consulting rates it charged clients for its consulting talent. The executive committee at BearingPoint was prepared to invest in a knowledge repository with technical e-training and certifications.

Internet learning as a component of all training and development at BearingPoint had increased from 0 percent in the beginning of 1999 to 65 percent at the end of 2002. The quality of courses remained consistent with a steady 4.2 rating over the years. The cost of delivering an hour of Internet-based learning had dropped from $48 per hour to $32 per hour. BearingPoint boasts an approach that is scalable and will eventually have all its corporate knowledge and learning needs met through online delivery.

The return on those investments was evident later when BearingPoint hired more than 1000 former employees of Arthur Anderson in July 2002. The company desired a fast and smooth assimilation to minimize stress and the learning curve for the employees. Using Internet learning, the employees were not only familiarized with the firm's methodologies and strategies, but they were also coached on the minute details of filling out HR forms and timesheets. The initiative allowed rapid transition, shorter time to billable hours, and targeted realization of contracts.

Nimble and Productive

As a group of 27 professionals, the Learning and Development organization ensured a positive contribution toward the company bottom line or top line on every dollar invested in Internet learning. The team ensures a consistent and common approach to learning and development at BearingPoint locations worldwide to reduce duplication of effort and offer predictability in the learner experience. The group defines learning as a combination of knowledge and experience.

The department maintains a lean organization relying on a program management office for managing Internet learning initiatives inside the organization. Key decisions regarding the program and objectives remain within the program management office, but the delivery, tools, and development functions are outsourced to providers. The team remains closely aligned with the regional business units to identify programmatic efforts. Regular meetings with the management committee of BearingPoint are held to assess and align learning priorities.

At BearingPoint, the delivery management functions rest with vendors. With a range of delivery options available, employees may choose from a host of synchronous or asynchronous learning solutions. With the ebb and flow of learning development volume at BearingPoint, the group advocates an outsourced model for delivery management. An outsourced model keeps internal overhead to a bare minimum while allowing flexibility in the content development process.

Besides reducing the need for an upfront financial commitment to initiate an Internet learning effort, outsourcing also offers a variety of development skills to an organization. Developing content for the Internet may well involve skills in instructional design, media graphics, web development, networking, and project management. Owning all the development skills needed to put together Internet learning content could make an initiative cost-prohibitive. Although outsourced, the development effort is coordinated through the program management office much like a consulting engagement with a project management schedule, defined deliverables, and a focus on budget.

Outsourcing the learning management services function, for instance, allows BearingPoint to receive timely reports for tracking employee development schedules and accomplishment without the need for deploying a specific application for BearingPoint.

What's in Store?

The favorable experience with Internet learning encouraged BearingPoint to continually leverage e-learning for its employees. The Learning and Development group at BearingPoint demonstrated how productivity and profitability benefits of e-learning were exponentially increased by turning what started out to be an internal project for the company into a robust solution for internal use and a new line of business.

The opportunity to converge voice, video, and data in a learning application will make the learning process even more engaging for learners. Although video over IP is desired, currently the network can handle only video on demand. Bandwidth considerations have limited the adoption of live video broadcasts through IP streaming.

To make learning even more relevant to the BearingPoint work force, skills enhancement should be complemented with motivation and vision. The team intends to leverage Internet learning to share top business talent within BearingPoint across all employees and consultants. Using synchronous and asynchronous web-based discussions, the team has launched a Leadership Series where C-level decision makers share best practices with consultants and employees on a regular basis.

Look Out, Land Mines Ahead

BearingPoint has advice for other oragizations planning an Internet learning deployment. The factors to watch out for include the following:

1. Lack of senior management sponsorship.

   An effort is doomed to fail if executive buy-in is limited or nonexistent. Without senior-level support, resistance to change will subvert even the most well-thought-through initiatives.

2. Technology is merely an enabler.

   Success of Internet learning is determined by factors other than technology. Responsive content, learner support, business operations, and clear objectives are critical factors that ensure a positive return on investment with Internet learning projects.

3. Reporting and analysis.

   An Internet learning effort should be supported with a strong reporting and analysis tool. Implementing a reporting tool may require system integration expertise.

Chapter 4: BearingPoint Makes a Grand Slam with Internet Learning

4 User experience.

If the learners ultimately are not satisfied with the content delivered, the project is bound to be short-lived. Focusing on user experience early in the development process is critical for subsequent success with Internet learning programs.

5 Cannot implement the demo.

Desirable features of an e-training or e-communication solution may not be feasible for implementation within an organization's network. Limitations such as those of bandwidth and performance in a network infrastructure should be considered to set manageable expectations among potential users.

Ways of Winning in the Enterprise

Based on BearingPoint's experience, the following are summarized as critical success factors:

1 Project Management 101.

Basic techniques of cost and time management can enable success in the learning space as well. Identifying red flags, such as production or development challenges, and addressing those before they turn into major hurdles can save organizational waste and delays.

2 Prototype and test.

Any solution that is intended for learner use should be put through a pilot process and rigorous testing for quality assurance. A deliberate and planned approach to development can ensure high-quality user experience at full-scale deployment.

3   Learn to operate with speed.

Line functions and business units operate on a timeline independent of learning processes. The learning functions must adapt to market, product, process, and economic changes to remain relevant and valuable to internal customers.

4   Eighty percent today is better than 100 percent never.

For internal customers, the timing for skills development, assessment, and enhancement is often a concern. If fine-tuning learning solutions might risk missing a market window, the quality risk is the one worth taking. Meeting the deadline with a learning solution that meets most of the learner needs, yet on time, will often be more meaningful to the customer than a fully baked solution that arrives too late.

Recommendations on Leading E-Learning

A study in the October 2002 issue of *Training* Magazine reported that of the 52-billion dollars spent on training in the United States, nearly 72 percent was spent on staff costs. At BearingPoint, the staff costs comprise about 20 percent of the total learning and development budget. Instructional design practices and systems integration practices essentially require similar skills. If training leaders commit to developing cost-effective approaches to delivering learning, they could well become key players in helping their organization's bottom line instead of remaining easy targets for budget cuts and layoffs.

When a training leader assumes the role of a CLO, there is a tacit agreement that instead of focusing on discrete training events he will leverage e-business tools to re-engineer the delivery of learning organization-wide. (See more on this in Chapter 14, "Practitioners' Views on the Business Advantages of E-Learning.") The team at Bearing Point contends that a training leader can preserve an organization's knowledge inventory despite budget reductions by relying on Internet learning. Instead of viewing their function as training and viewing themselves as trainers, today's training managers should view learning as a business-transformation opportunity and view themselves as change agents.

Conclusion

The chapter demonstrated a business-process-optimization view taken by BearingPoint when integrating core components of e-learning into the organization's learning environment. BearingPoint deployed e-communication, e-training, and e-assessment to respond to its changing business needs with good effect. The organization assumed a management approach toward e-learning that established the learning organization's role as a vibrant support entity for the entire organization.

CHAPTER 5

LEARNER DRIVEN AT THE UNIVERSITY OF TOYOTA: PIONEERS OF JUST-IN-TIME ADVOCATE "HANDS-ON" SKILLS

> ### Key Take-Away
>
> In addition to being a viable business strategy, just-in-time learning and learner-driven content at Toyota has been in constant demand and has, therefore, made outsourcing imperative.

Supporting staff with skills development in nontechnical subject matter, often referred to as *soft skills*, and using a combination of knowledge sharing, training, and assessment make a valid case for Internet learning deployment in nontechnical verticals. The University of Toyota appears to have leveraged a productivity pyramid metaphor much like Cisco to create a smarter work force by offering employees flexibility in learning choices and by playing to their strengths.

Case Summary

The adoption of an integrated learning approach among companies, consciously or unconsciously, suggests its usefulness to those who seek workforce development. Development, maintenance, and assessment of soft skills are key components of a learner-driven performance-improvement system at Toyota. According to Ellie Tymer, Associate Dean of the University of Toyota, boosting productivity among U.S.-based Toyota employees is based on delivering content with an emphasis on access, control, and relevance to learners. Aside from making it just-in-time, Toyota makes learning "hands on" by using innovative content based on a cost-effective business model.

Background

Based in Los Angeles, California, the University of Toyota meets the needs of 9000 Toyota employees, who are commonly referred to as *associates*, and resellers nationwide. The organization follows a university metaphor with titles such as Dean and Associate Dean to represent executive and senior management tiers within the university. The programs offered at the university can be broadly

Chapter 5: Learner Driven at the University of Toyota

categorized as those for the dealer or reseller network and those for employees, or associates. Because the primary roles of Toyota's U.S. associates are sales, marketing, customer service, and administration, the essential content aimed for development of associates primarily deals with soft skills.

Ellie Tymer is responsible for delivering just-in-time, relevant, and accessible anytime-and-anywhere content to associates. Tymer believes that if associates understand the relevance of how learning a certain skill set can improve their productivity and performance, they are more likely to engage in learning. In her opinion, the primary goal of a learning organization should be to demonstrate the value of learning and follow it up with access to tools so that learners find the pursuit of learning easy.

Just-in-Time Learning: A Business Function at Toyota

For those at the University of Toyota, learning is a tool for solving business problems. When they hit an impasse, associates have the option to access an electronic learning tool that enables them to perform a specific task—ranging from creating project plans to preparing a presentation—through self-driven modules. To complement the learning tool, associates can access an on-demand tutor to assist with solving the problem at hand. According to Tymer, the relevance of such learning to one's job is almost perfect.

By aligning learning with performance, the University of Toyota acts as a business function that facilitates the productivity of the core business functions, such as sales and manufacturing, also referred to as *line functions*. Supporting sales and marketing organizations through a just-in-time approach to training and development makes learning just as indispensable a function as technical support or billing functions for the associates working at Toyota.

Cost-Effective Business Model

Through an outsourced approach to content creation, the University of Toyota keeps its content library current and relevant at a fraction of what it might have cost for the company itself to create it. It places the responsibility of investing in content with an expert external organization instead of internally with Toyota. The university has a relationship with ElementK for an e-training curriculum that features access to more than 700 IT technical and desktop applications serving 4500 registered learners through elementk.com on topics ranging from personal computing to web design. According to Tymer, the response to an outsourced e-training curriculum has been "phenomenal."

An outsourced content library has also strengthened the just-in-time proposition that is critical to the university's offerings. Tymer recalls a situation in which a manager was to present his graphs and charts on Microsoft Project—a tool with which he and his team were not familiar with—at a meeting the next day. By enrolling in a self-paced e-Learning course that same day, the manager and his team quickly acquired the skills to convert the presentation. The support was timely, accessible, and relevant for the team. Through anytime-anyplace access to learning, a potential showstopper was averted, and the presentation proceeded without a hitch.

As an evaluation metric, Toyota uses a return-on-expectations assessment to determine the cost-effectiveness and cost-efficiency of its performance-improvement efforts. By gathering feedback from customer departments, the University of Toyota determines how its role affects productivity among other organizations. This form of evaluation provides input for analysis of learning and development programs.

Even "Know-It-Alls" Can't Escape

Carrying its reliance on electronic learning tools further, Toyota has adopted the use of simulations for skills development and assessment. By allowing individuals to acquire and demonstrate skills through "hands-on" simulations that are based on real-life scenarios, the university has increased the performance impact of e-learning at Toyota.

Chapter 5: Learner Driven at the University of Toyota

Before setting out to acquire new skills in areas of customer service, for example, a learner can choose to go through a simulation-based assessment item. The assessment might offer a case of an irate customer with a complaint. The questions posed by the assessment vary based on the previous responses of the learner. Eventually, the tool culminates the scenario with an "outcome"—desirable or undesirable—to inform the learner of his customer service prowess. Through the outcome, the learner receives valuable hints with regard to areas of improvement and skills development.

The hands-on nature of these simulation tools makes them a useful option for blended learning as well. Even in classroom settings, learners can assess and develop their skills by using simulation tools. Through a hand-in-hand combination of assessment and development, simulations offer a low-risk means of employee development in an environment that approximates a real-life scenario.

The University of Toyota has contracted with SkillSoft for 200 such simulation-based development and assessment modules in the areas of customer service, finance, negotiation skills, business writing, and management. By leveraging an existing library from a vendor, Toyota can adopt unique simulation tools without bearing the cost of development.

Deploying a Productivity Cycle at Toyota

Deploying a productivity cycle at Toyota involves an eight-step process that ensures that that employee learning translates into productivity advantages for the organization. (See Figure 5-1.)

Figure 5-1 *Performance Improvement Cycle*

**Personal and Professional Productivity
Performance Improvement Cycle
University of Toyota**

Step 1	Step 2	Step 3	Step 4
Confirmation of Learning Objectives	Leadership Alignment	Participant Preparation	Learning Session
Participants will be able to identify objectives that meet their learning needs	Supports The Toyota Way's corner-stone of 'Lean Thinking' as well as the Corporate Vision	Identify performance gaps and talent enhancement opportunities	Implement learning

Step 5	Step 6	Step 7	Step 8
Workplace Re-Entry	On-Going Support	Measuring Progress	Future Development Planning
Share action plan with sponsors to ensure learning is applied on the job	Review progress with accountability partner and sponsor. On-going development discussions with sponsor	Electronic evaluations used to gather data on class effectiveness in terms of the materials, facilitators, and learning objectives	Selected Development Opportunities. Reassess skills and learning plan using Continuum Step 3

Chapter 5: Learner Driven at the University of Toyota

The eight steps are as follows:

Step 1. Confirmation of learning objectives—When developing learning plans, an individual's talents play a key role in determining learning objectives. Toyota's approach to development is based on the individual's strengths. Associates are encouraged to draft their own goals as to which skills or tactics might improve their performance even further. Rather than offering training to eliminate weaknesses so that all individuals can possess skills at par with a predetermined benchmark, the University of Toyota's culture encourages playing to individual strengths. By building on existing talents, the organization allows individuals to excel in their domain.

Step 2. Leadership alignment—The individual's manager reviews the learning objectives to ensure that they meet corporate direction and vision. After the objectives are reviewed and found to be in alignment, they are incorporated into the development plan. The manager supports the learning objective by coaching and encouraging self-assessment.

Step 3. Participant preparation—Based on an online pre-assessment, the learner can identify strengths and weaknesses in the skill area. By comparing current strengths with the learning objectives, a learner develops an individual learning plan. The learning plan turns into a "learning contract" in consultation with the manager. A learning contract is a document that serves to guide what an individual might learn on the job. The learning contract, in turn, is included in the individual's performance appraisal.

Step 4. Learning session—During the learning session, the learner gathers new skills. With an accountability partner at the University of Toyota, the learner sets certain follow-up commitments, including using electronic modules on the topic that continue beyond the learning session.

Step 5. Workplace re-entry—Upon completing the learning session, the learner creates an action plan to incorporate the newly learned job skills into real-life work. Over the course of the next few weeks, through the use of tutors or e-modules, the learner refines the use of newly acquired skills and applies the practices on the job.

Step 6. Ongoing support—The learner reviews the progress with the manager and explores approaches that might prove useful in deploying the newly acquired skills into her real-life work.

Step 7. Measuring progress—Thirty days after the learning session, the accountability partner from the University of Toyota follows up on the action plan to assess the extent to which newly acquired skills were incorporated on the job. The learner completes electronic evaluations to provide feedback on learning effectiveness through learning objectives. The learner also retakes the original online assessment to identify changes in strengths and weaknesses as a result of the learning process.

Step 8. Future development planning—Based on the original assessment in Step 3, the learner identifies development opportunities and new skill areas to pursue. The process continues with a review of current skills and development of a new learning contract with the manager.

Conclusion

Through a combination of e-assessment and e-training, the University of Toyota has demonstrated success in imparting soft skills to its diverse workforce across the United States at low cost with anytime-anywhere access. In addition to being a viable business strategy, the constant demand for just-in-time learning and learner-driven content at Toyota has made outsourcing imperative. By allowing other organizations to develop the customized content, the University of Toyota can provide its associates with the latest and most relevant e-training delivery and deployment tools.

CHAPTER 6

E-LEARNING GOES GLOBAL: NETWORKING ACADEMY TRANSFORMS LIVES

The Business Case for E-Learning

> *Key Take-Away*
>
> The creation, rapid growth, and global presence of a massive networking talent pool trained via the Cisco Networking Academy Program would not have been possible without a solid e-learning strategy.

Never before have learning and education been as accessible as they are now over the Internet. Today, education can cross boundaries and reach the far-flung corners of the planet. It is now possible, via the Internet, to share technology, best practices, and information, making time and space barriers essentially transparent. If the Internet and education are indeed the two greatest equalizers, the Cisco Networking Academy Program has leveled the playing field for thousands of individuals worldwide with its Internet learning model.

Case Summary

The Cisco Networking Academy Program offers an example of social investment, Internet learning, and educational problem solving in one case study. The program partners with more than 10,000 educational institutions located in more than 140 countries worldwide to deliver technology instruction to upward of 400,000 students. It offers a classic model of leveraging the components of an integrated learning approach—e-communication, e-training, and e-assessment—to change lives, empower institutions, and strengthen the foundation of networking talent globally.

Background

George Ward, a Cisco Senior Engineer, developed training for teachers and staff for maintenance of school networks. He traveled around the country conducting his training sessions and discovered that although schools were being wired and connected to the Internet, they lacked financial and human resources to manage and maintain networks. He felt that it was difficult to expect instructors teaching a course to rely on networks if they did not have a way to support them.

George started training the students at these institutions in school-network maintenance. The success of student seminars led to requests from participating schools across the United States for Cisco to develop a curriculum that could be integrated into an instructor-led class as an elective course taught in a semester format. Cisco management realized that a curriculum could best be delivered across multiple sites using Internet learning.

The formalized curriculum and support activities evolved into the Cisco Networking Academy Program. The program was launched in October 1997, with 64 academies in 7 U.S. states. This program was created to support schools and academic institutions that did not have IT or networking support centers and to teach students how to design, build, and maintain computer networks at their schools. Through Internet learning, the project could be scaled, if the demand warranted, without the overhead of travel and time commitments.

In just seven years, the program (a partnership between corporate, government, and individuals) demonstrated how the Internet can transform education by leveraging an Internet learning model that works. Through a combination of e-communication, e-training, and e-assessment tools, the Academy delivers its curriculum to countries around the world. The program also supports nearly 20,000 instructors through an e-learning instructor-readiness program. Through the Cisco Networking Academy Program, more than 6000 educational institutions around the world have implemented e-learning.

With more than 100,000 graduates already in the field with an estimated 50 percent employed in the industry, the Networking Academy has created a valuable talent pool for employers to tap into for recruitment. The remaining 50 percent choose to pursue further education or other careers. Wherever the networking industry experiences a labor shortage around the globe, the program delivers a steady flow of qualified, certified candidates.

How the Program Works

The Networking Academy Program offers a comprehensive blended e-learning solution that provides students technology instruction in traditional classroom settings worldwide. High schools, community colleges, and universities serve as academies to the program delivering technical content to its students. A global e-learning infrastructure delivers all the learning components to more than 10,000 academies worldwide. The learning components include web-based content, online assessments, student performance tracking, hands-on-labs, and instructor training and support. The learning tools help prepare students for Cisco and other IT certifications.

Industry-Responsive Curriculum

To graduate from the program, a students needs to pass the assessments offered during the four-semester program. Pursuing a Cisco or other IT certification is optional, not a mandatory requirement of the program. Initially created to prepare students for the Cisco Certified Network Associate (CCNA) and Cisco Certified Network Professional (CCNP) degrees, the Academy curriculum has expanded with other IT sponsored courses. Some of the available courses are Fundamentals of Web Design, sponsored by Adobe Systems; IT Essentials: PC Hardware and Software, and IT Essentials: Network Operating Systems, sponsored by Hewlett-Packard; Fundamentals of Voice and Data Cabling, sponsored by Panduit; and Fundamentals of UNIX and Fundamentals of Java, sponsored by Sun Microsystems.

Train-the-Trainer Model

The program relies on a train-the-trainer model that is supported by the e-learning infrastructure. Cisco Systems trains 50 Cisco Academy Training Centers (CATCs) around the world that serve as lead training organizations. The CATCs help train regional instructors on the Networking Academy curriculum delivery and approach. Regional academies assume a leadership role by not only delivering content to their own students, but by also supporting a host of smaller neighboring local academies. The regional academies train the local academy instructors. These local academies offer classes on site to students. Because all the materials are readily available on-line, the train-the-trainer model complements the e-learning infrastructure in ensuring that the instructors are well supported.

Blended Learning with E-Assessment

An important component of the program is creating assessment tasks that are tightly aligned with the curriculum. The program relies on instructors in the field to generate and validate assessment items. Pre-test, practice, and post-test tools are made available to students in the program through the e-learning infrastructure. In addition to formal testing with scoring and grade books, students can also receive feedback on their skill and knowledge acquisition through chapter quizzes embedded in the curriculum as well as hands-on skill-focused exams given by instructors.

Assessment provides students with performance feedback. A personalized feedback report provides a single source of content links that helps the student quickly navigate through the curriculum for test review or further study. Proficiency reports enable students to translate the numeric value of their assessment into some level of proficiency, such as Novice, Partially Proficient, Proficient, or Advanced. Because the reports include direct links to an online version of the curriculum, the e-learning infrastructure automatically determines, and links to, the most efficient source on the network to provide students personalized and relevant material for review. The program uses a database and statistical models to monitor and maintain tests that instructors use in the classroom. Through this effort, the program offers leadership in best practices regarding test design and maintenance to help both students and teachers in the classroom.

Much of the success of the Networking Academy Program has been attributed to its hands-on nature. Developers working on the Cisco Networking Academy Program have integrated simulations into the curriculum that provide students with an exciting, virtual, hands-on experience. Students are required to work through more than 200 labs. Most of these labs include extensive technical configuration. Simulations provide students an opportunity for additional virtual practice to increase the effectiveness of hands-on lab time.

Underserved Segment

The Cisco Networking Academy Program also works to help population segments that might have been left behind in the digital economy because of a lack of access to technology. The program offers programs in underserved areas to benefit low-income individuals, certain ethnic groups, people in disadvantaged communities, and those with disabilities. Academies located in underserved communities and countries help local people learn the IT skills they need to acquire to sustain technology growth in the region.

Impact of the Program

Regardless of race, gender, culture, or socioeconomic status, individuals worldwide are engaged in building a better future through the Cisco Networking Academy Program, which helps communities transcend the digital divide of information "haves" and "have-nots." As part of their project-based learning activities, students have a chance to give back to their communities by designing, building, and maintaining networks for local schools and other civic organizations. At the same time, it provides educational institutions with in-house resources to manage their technology. It provides invaluable preparation for college coursework in science, math, and engineering (as well as for employment in the IT field).

Richard Murnane, Professor of Education and Society at Harvard, submitted a study, "Can the Internet Help Solve America's Education Problems: Lessons from the Cisco Networking Academies" (with N. Sharkey and F. Levy), to the National Research Council (NRC), an arm of the National Academy of Sciences. This study looked at how the program works, why it appeals to high schools and community colleges, and how the academy team dealt with problems that they confronted in schools and, in particular, how it made use of information technology in crafting solutions. The authors believe that the Cisco Networking Academy Program and its development provides valuable insights into how to address the challenges of the American education system and the role of the Internet in providing solutions to those challenges. The authors believe that Internet learning can

- Address skill needs in the education sector
- Find quality teachers and provide ongoing professional development
- Create equal-education opportunities for all

In a recent article in the *Harvard Business Review* (December 2002), "The Competitive Advantage of Corporate Philanthropy," Michael Porter and Mark Kramer wrote that the program "exemplifies the powerful links that exist between a company's philanthropic strategy, its competitive context and social benefits." It mentions that Cisco has created a program that "no other educational institution, government agency, foundation, or corporate donor could have designed as well or expanded as rapidly." Discussing the benefits of the program to Cisco, the article mentions that besides strengthening its market share and providing employers in the technology industry with hundreds of qualified employees, the program has helped Cisco increase "the sophistication of its customers."

Benefits to Cisco

So where is the value for Cisco in this effort? A list of values follows:

- Value of philanthropy

    The program offers a social investment of global magnitude that offers an opportunity for those who are willing to help themselves. According to the Council of Foundations (in 2002), nearly four out of five shareholders will reinvest when a company has a high Corporate Philanthropic Index (CPI). Having a high CPI contributes toward higher customer loyalty and even higher employee loyalty.

- Government relations

    With its global recognition, the Cisco Networking Academy Program helps establish contact and extend relationships with top government leaders worldwide. The program positions Cisco as a leader in both Internet technologies and education.

- Ecosystem

    The partnerships and the talent pool generated through the Networking Academy Program help strengthen the ecosystem around Cisco, and the Cisco strategic partners and resellers value the commitment that Cisco has made to workforce development through the program.

- Model for Internet learning

  The Cisco Networking Academy is a living example of how Internet learning continues to enable expansion of the program. Through its high-growth period, with 50 to 100 academies being set up almost every week, the Internet learning offered an expansion mechanism that would not have been sustainable through traditional learning delivery. Because of its impact on various schools and community colleges worldwide, administrators in educational institutions now consider Internet learning a viable educational delivery means for other curricula as well.

- Internet learning in the "traditional classroom"

  The Networking Academy Program demonstrates a model of how e-learning can equip instructors with subject matter expertise, assessment tools, and learning management support even in the traditional classroom. Using its global e-learning infrastructure, Cisco Networking Academy delivers content to its instructors, ensuring consistency of content and assessment items. The model is unique and offers insight to organizations seeking to deliver educational or training content to geographically dispersed audiences in traditional classroom settings as well.

Changing Lives One Life at a Time

After the genocide in Rwanda in 1994, the social fabric of the nation shifted dramatically, with women having to take lead economic roles to fend for their families. According to the Global Fund for Women, in the wake of the genocide, women now constitute approximately 70 percent of Rwanda's population, and 50 percent of these women are widows. Rwanda Ministry of Gender has helped many women acquire skills, identify markets, and start small businesses. The ministry encourages workers to identify and acquire new skills to assist women to improve their economic well-being. Cisco Networking Academy played a role in one such effort to disseminate technical know-how in Rwanda.

Beth Murora, a program officer at the National Rwandan Ministry of Women's Affairs, received a scholarship to attend the Networking Academy Program. The program was being offered in Addis Ababa, Ethiopia, nearly 1000 miles from her home in Kigali, Rwanda. Beth had been accepted into a Networking

Academy Program pilot project sponsored by Cisco Systems, the United Nations Economic Commission for Africa (UNECA), and the World Bank's Information for Development Program (InfoDev). The Networking Academy Program in Ethiopia was part of the Least Developed Countries (LDC) initiative, which has brought the Networking Academy Program to 31 of the world's 49 LDCs. The program was delivered through a blended-learning solution, where the instructors receive content and assessment tools through an e-learning component but deliver classes in person to students attending the program.

To participate in the Networking Academy Program, Beth had to leave her family for six months, during which time she became a mother of twin boys. "It was one of the most difficult decisions of my life," recalls Beth. "But, too often women lose opportunities to advance themselves because of family obligations. I could not pass up this opportunity, which would help me to help other women in Rwanda. I had a vision and the willingness to make it a reality."

"I wanted to be part of this program," says Beth. "It bridged both gender and digital divides—issues that are of concern to me. And it had the potential to empower women with information technology skills that lead to economic opportunities. Such empowerment is critical for Rwandan women." With the assurances that nutritional, medical, and transportation needs would be met and the guarded support of her husband and family, Beth embarked on her journey to Ethiopia accompanied by her mother-in-law. "I knew my babies would be in good hands while I attended classes," recalls Beth.

Participation in the Academy Program was fully supported by the National Rwandan Ministry of Women's Affairs. The minister of the Rwandan Ministry of Women's Affairs worked with the Rwandan embassy in Addis Ababa to ensure that Beth's medical and housing needs would be taken care of while she attended the Academy Program.

With a bachelor degree in public administration from the National University of Rwanda, Beth had but a few computer-related courses under her belt. She knew that the Networking Academy Program, which follows the 280-hour, 6-month Cisco Certified Network Associate (CCNA) curriculum, would pose a challenge. In addition, through the UNECA African Center for Women, Academy Program participants were trained in gender and development, entrepreneurship, and management skills.

"Some days it was very hard for me," says Beth. "But the Networking Academy instructors were very helpful. They kept me going and encouraged me to succeed. I set out of my country with a goal to achieve. Despite the pains I felt some mornings, by sheer force of will I got out of bed and to my classes because of my goal. By accomplishing what I set out to do, I knew I could look forward to much happiness when I returned to my home—mission accomplished, and with my new babies."

Achieve her missions she did. In October 2001, Beth gave birth to two healthy boys, and in February 2002, Beth completed her CCNA coursework. Upon her joyous return to Rwanda, Beth possessed a networking and IT skill set enabling her to pursue the development and implementation of technology programs championed by the Rwandan Ministry of Gender.

"The genocide left a country in need of rebuilding, both physically and emotionally," says Beth. "The majority of Rwandan women are single mothers and very, very poor. These women must be able to earn a living and support their children. And I intend to use the knowledge gained through the Networking Academy to help raise women out of poverty with the technical training to run organizations and develop businesses, and a communications network that enables information sharing among women forums."

Conclusion

With its global success in transforming lives, learning, and social paradigms, the Cisco Networking Academy Program is hailed as a remarkably successful example of a productivity pyramid metaphor. The program's rapid acceleration, global presence, and creation of a massive networking talent pool would not have been possible without Internet learning. The case study presents a strong argument that global delivery of content can best be achieved through astute deployment of Internet learning in combination with existing classroom instruction. Solid strategy and process-driven results can be achieved even by making Internet learning a complementary component of the existing learning structure.

CHAPTER 7

TARGETED LEARNING: ARE YOU *INDEED* READY?

> ### Key Take-Away
> By closely aligning with business objectives, individual strengths, and targeted learning plans, a skills-gap approach to work-force development can help make the cohesive learning effort an integral part of the business process.

Case Summary

Using a competency-development process, the Cisco sales organization launched a portal called MyDevelopment that measures the readiness of the sales force given current sales objectives. The tools help to assess each salesperson's individual strengths and weaknesses with respect to her targets and offers targeted learning plans. MyDevelopment provides a formal approach for creating an individualized learning model based on need for each employee in the sales organization.

The synthesis of e-communication, e-training, and e-assessment tools for employee development can be planned and measured through an automated process for managing individual productivity. Cisco sought a process for individuals to administer and control their learning by tying it to skills, with success metrics. The answer: MyDevelopment.

The MyDevelopment tool created by the Cisco sales force development team demonstrates the use of a web-based tool that helps tie productivity improvement efforts with the sales planning process to achieve targeted learning.

Rationale Behind Targeted Learning

How common is it in organizations for an executive to be up on a stage at a sales rally and make a commitment to achieve success with a product? But ask the same executive how ready the sales team is to meet the challenge of selling that product, and you will receive vague responses.

An organization's common approach in such situations is to resort to "blanket training"—that is, train the entire sales force on a specific product or technology and hope that everyone on the team will be ready to meet the sales objectives. However, a blanket training approach might be a waste of resources in regions with different levels of market need or readiness. Besides, a blanket approach could lead to overtraining in some areas and undertraining in others. What if the productivity bottleneck in the case of an individual is not so much product knowledge, but more interpersonal skills? By offering training that is not individualized to the needs of a salesperson, the organization risks allocating training dollars toward developing a salesperson on unnecessary skill sets.

The alternative to blanket training is targeted learning. Targeted learning means developing people based on their specific skill needs for their current performance objective. Cisco has accomplished targeted learning through MyDevelopment with individualized targeted learning plans for the sales force to strengthen their intended skill areas.

Targeted learning is about having management's finger on the pulse of sales force readiness. If management can determine how well each salesperson measures up against what he needs to know to be successful, they can intelligently recommend individualized programs for sales readiness.

From "Best Trained" to "Most Competent"

In 2002, Cisco was rated the best-trained sales force in the entire industry in the U.S. by *Sales and Marketing Management* Magazine. As if being labeled the "best trained" in the press was not sufficient, Cisco management set a goal for its sales force to also be the most competent in the industry. To articulate the learning imperative at Cisco, Chuck Battipede, Director of Operations, Worldwide Sales Force Development Group, coined the motto: "Respected by its customers, feared by its competitors."

The Sales Force Development Group wanted to ensure that each individual in the sales force had the skills required to meet his own sales targets. To achieve this end, a targeted learning plan for each salesperson had to be customized based on the salesperson's skill needs with respect to the current year's sales objectives. For example, the level of detail in training would vary between what a sales engineer is expected to know about a solution versus what an account manager is expected to know. Similarly, if two markets experience demand for the same solution, the demographics, customer needs, and competitive structures in different territories might compel the sales force to develop differing skill sets.

A targeted learning approach to skills and competence development is expected to make sales force development more timely, need based, and sales driven. The approach will cause the limited learning budgets to be used in delivering direct benefits to Cisco revenue and profits. In the words of Chuck Battipede, Director of Operations, the approach allows Cisco to set its sales force "development goals, which clearly impact their ability to perform well on their current jobs in the short-term." According to Battipede, the targeted learning approach is a key strategic advantage that "few competitors will be able to replicate easily."

The Development Cycle: A Three-Step Process

The following steps describe the development cycle process in more detail. A salesperson is expected to follow the steps to meet her learning objectives:

Step 1. Complete assessment on MyDevelopment.

>To identify her existing skill level, the individual completes a series of assessment forms on each attribute that is needed for success. The attributes might include product knowledge, technology know-how, deployment expertise, presentation skills, or interpersonal skills. Based on existing skill level and needed skill level for the job, the system identifies the skills gap.
>
>After the assessment process is complete and the skills gap identified, MyDevelopment notifies the line manager about the skills gaps. Beyond the skills gaps identified by the process, the line manager may further dictate priorities that are considered desirable for success.

Chapter 7: Targeted Learning: Are You Indeed Ready?

Step 2. Derive a targeted learning plan.

Based on the skills-gap analysis, the MyDevelopment tool prepares a targeted learning plan. The learning plan taps into the available e-communication, e-training, and e-assessment tools to create a customized learning path for an individual to follow.

The learning plan also provides a short list of recommended training, knowledge sharing, and certification options for the individual to pursue. By offering automatic learning steps to pursue, the tool saves the salesperson the effort of looking through a list of classes and guessing which courses can help him meet the skills gaps. At Cisco, classroom courses, white papers, online learning, and *video on demand (VoD)* mapped to the individual's skills needs are all available to the sales force through the MyDevelopment portal.

Step 3. Take action.

The individual is expected to follow the required the MyDevelopment portal's recommendations. Using the SFCD portal involves the following three steps:

Assessment—Assess yourself objectively and realistically.

Learning plan—Develop a learning plan with your manager.

Learning—Take the training and use what you learn.

As one progresses toward completing the suggested learning plan, management can track the development of the individual toward desired competencies.

After the targeted skill and proficiency levels have been achieved, a sales manager may be confident in the knowledge that the team has the potential to meet the original goals head-on. Each quarter or year as sale's targets and thus its targeted skills change, the desired performance attributes are altered. By using the MyDevelopment tool, the teams can allocate training resources on pinpointed skill sets.

Learning Portals for Productivity: Facilitating the Manager

As a business tool and process, skills-gap analysis efforts stand to generate substantial productivity advantages. A unique element of the process is how closely line managers are tied to the development efforts undertaken by their teams. Because line managers have a vested interest in their teams' success, the approach creates automatic organizational buy-in for learning within the organization.

A portal such as MyDevelopment, deployed by Cisco Sales Force Development, generates output that is useful to managers for work-force development decision making without the additional paperwork and other cumbersome activities.

Following is the list of outputs from the process flow that a portal might generate for business-focused implementation of a skills- and competency-based development effort. (See Figure 7-1.)

Figure 7-1 *Overall Impact on Business*

Chapter 7: Targeted Learning: Are You Indeed Ready?

1. Selection of success attributes.

   To begin, managers can identify key business drivers and priorities within an organization and select the attributes against which employees are to assess themselves.

   For example, a senior manager responsible for sales forces development in *Europe, the Middle East, and Africa (EMEA)* might be faced with distinct product training needs for each of the submarkets. The senior manager in this example might decide to focus on advanced technologies in the Western European markets, core technologies in Eastern European markets, solution selling in Middle Eastern markets, and new product introductions in Africa.

2. Prioritization and forecasting by territory.

   The analysis should enable management to prioritize and forecast by territory, identifying spending against development and rapid response to changes within each region of the organization.

   In the example of training in EMEA, the prioritization would translate into making decisions about what type e-communication, e-training, and e-assessment tools are needed in each of the markets, the number of users expected for each of the tools, and the speed of implementation in each of the markets. Accordingly, decisions around budgets and delivery timelines for learning tools would depend on such analysis.

3. Progress review.

   Management can retrieve reports to see the skills trends within the overall organization.

   Because each of the markets in this example have distinct learning objectives, the senior manager can retrieve learning successes achieved by the sales force in each of the markets and measure progress against the business objectives for that particular region.

4. Input into individual learning plans.

   Combining a development forecast with territory priorities and seeing the overall analysis of an organization, managers should be able to assign learning that ensures that they have reached the team or departmental goals.

The tool offers the capability to drill down to the individual level to provide insight into any deviations from the plan. The senior manager can adjust the strategy or allocate more resources toward implementation of the learning tools by reviewing the progress of specific individuals, if needed.

5. Determine a *return on investment (ROI)* on learning.

    After the team has completed its targeted learning plans and has been applying their knowledge and skills, managers can assess the ROI and use those results to influence future business decisions and priorities.

    Six months or a year into the implementation, the senior manager in our example of EMEA can determine the improvement in the visibility and improved sales of products and solutions based on each of the markets. Customer satisfaction numbers, feedback from the sales personnel, and feedback from sales leadership can offer useful input into quantifying the improvement specific learning initiatives have made in each of the regions.

Conclusion

Using a skills-gap approach to developing targeted learning plans, Cisco has created a model for improving sales force readiness. When linked to experience and performance management, the model can also be used for long-term workforce development in engineering, manufacturing, support, as well as sales. By closely aligning with business objectives, individual strengths, and targeted learning plans, a skills-gap approach to work-force development can help make the productivity pyramid an integral part of the business process.

CHAPTER 8

PRODUCTIVITY IN THE EXTENDED ENTERPRISE: INTERNET LEARNING OFFERS A COMPETITIVE EDGE WITH CHANNEL PARTNERS

The Business Case for E-Learning

Lisa Baumert, manager of marketing programs in the Customer Advocacy Group of Cisco Systems, coauthored this chapter.

Key Take-Away

Access to skills development, skills maintenance, and skills-assessment tools differentiates between vendors in the channel environment. With e-learning, channel partners can tap into a vendor knowledge base just as effectively as a direct sales force—anytime, anyplace.

In the fast-changing vertical of information technology, the extended sales force of partners and reseller organizations needs to keep pace with technological and product developments just like the internal sales force. An *extended enterprise*, as a term, refers to all employees across a chain of suppliers and resellers who influence the eventual use and adoption of a product. The cost of skills development using traditional training techniques can be cost-prohibitive. The case study presented here describes the Cisco Systems approach to e-learning, which reduces the cost of developing a channel program for both the vendor and the reseller.

Case Summary

By using Internet learning, Cisco not only improved partner satisfaction with its reseller program, but also established a competitive advantage, which has differentiated Cisco and improved partner effectiveness. Employees in the reseller channel will often best represent products and services from manufacturers that offer the greatest level of support and reseller satisfaction in terms of knowledge and guidance on features and solutions. The importance of a healthy, successful channel is critical in the marketplace. Cisco is focused on maintaining a cohesive, effective, and profitable channel. Learning is an essential part of the relationship between Cisco and its partner organizations.

The Value Proposition

Cisco realized an annual savings of $142 million in fiscal year 2003 (discussed in Chapter 3, "E-Learning Under the Microscope") from Internet learning, which included $41 million generated in savings through the development of a partner portal, the *Partner E-Learning Connection (PEC)*. A later study conducted in April 2004 demonstrated that PEC generated $16 for every dollar spent on it during the course of fiscal year 2003. (See Chapter 3 for a complete analysis.)

A nonmeasurable benefit of this tool is the value and competitive advantages that accrue to Cisco partners and resellers by deploying a comprehensive Internet learning system including assessment, training, and knowledge sharing for partners. The increased success that Cisco has experienced with the partner program through e-learning for partner employees underscores the business advantages of empowering not just the immediate, but also the extended workforce of an organization—its partner and reseller channel.

A Program That Rewards Learning

The nature of the Cisco Partner Specialization program (discussed in Chapter 10, "Certifications as a Branding Tool: Sponsoring a Certification Program") places a premium on skills and learning. The Cisco Partner Specialization is a program that helps Cisco reseller organizations acquire expertise in specific lines of products and services through learning, exams, and certifications. The program relies heavily on meeting learning goals. Developing career-certified individuals, obtaining specialization points, and pursuing extra credits are all possible through an effort to continually increase organizational learning and maintain a higher level of knowledge than the competition. The policies help to generate an ongoing demand for lifelong learning in Cisco partner channels among 25,000 companies employing more than 500,000 individuals globally in more than 130 countries. Based on their skills, partners accumulate points, which eventually determine their discount rates with Cisco. With discount rates at stake, the motivation among partners to assimilate knowledge creates an inherent demand for learning. If such a demand is not adequately addressed through a complementary learning program, the lack of learning opportunities can easily turn into low satisfaction toward Cisco among channel members. (For more on this, see Chapter 10.)

The Learning Challenge

In February 2000, the training required to meet the learning goals of reseller organizations worldwide were woefully inadequate in terms of quantity of classes offered and regional availability of courses. The challenge of keeping partner organizations current on hundreds of complex products evolving every six to nine months was a daunting and formidable task.

Systems engineers and account managers from Cisco spent an inordinate amount of their time flying from one partner headquarter to another with labs, equipment, and training materials to inform and educate partners on technologies and solutions. An approach of delivering all the instruction face to face ended up requiring repeated training sessions for each product before it reached a worldwide audience. Despite the best efforts of these systems engineers, it was estimated that mission-critical training content reached less than 5 percent of the employees in Cisco partner organizations.

Systems engineers would often conduct knowledge-sharing sessions, in Cisco offices, to cover the fundamental elements of technology behind a product. This effort to conduct training on products was taking time from their core responsibilities of business development.

Unable to obtain timely information, Cisco resellers often resorted to multiple sources of information on product and service features, which created inconsistencies and disparities in product and service knowledge across reseller organizations. Lack of adequate training and certification support was beginning to negatively impact customer satisfaction among partner employees. With increasing competitive pressure, the learning challenges became a contributing factor to channel dissatisfaction.

PEC: A Viable Learning Solution

Based on success that Cisco had experienced with its *Field E-Learning Connection (FELC)* for supporting the learning needs of the direct sales force, Cisco leveraged the model of a learning portal to its extended enterprise comprised of partner organizations. In March 2000, Cisco created a one-stop,

Chapter 8: PRODUCTIVITY in the Extended Enterprise

application-based learning portal called *Partner E-Learning Connection (PEC)*, which met most partner learning needs through relevant content about products, services, and technologies. As an Internet learning solution, PEC was able to offer each employee within its partner companies personalized access to content, thereby meeting the needs of the specific individual. (See Figure 8-1.)

If a new product is launched that was relevant to only one individual at an overseas branch of a U.S. reseller, that specific individual can find support online when learning about that product. She can pull up the slides, review the accompanying notes, listen to the *video-on-demand (VoD)* presentation, and review white papers on the topic—all from the portal—to gather in-depth understanding of the product.

Figure 8-1   Learning Preference

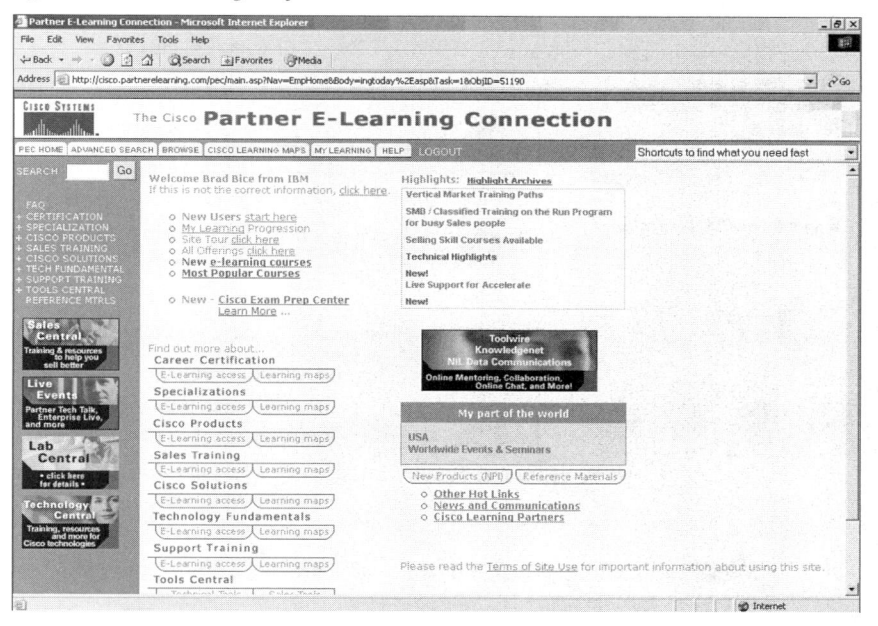

The portal continues to expand its offering in e-training, e-communication, and e-assessment tools. Learners can pursue a formal curriculum as well as obtain specific information on products and technologies. Practice tools and assessment items enable learners to validate their skills or prepare for certifications. Some common features of the PEC include the following:

- A robust search and browse functionality that scans disparate databases and systems at Cisco to find VoD modules that are relevant to a learner's focus, subject matter, speaker, or sales theater anywhere in the world.

- Learning maps that group course offerings around a common learning objective together with navigation tools linking directly to the courses. (See Figure 8-2.)

Figure 8-2 *Learning Maps for Resellers*

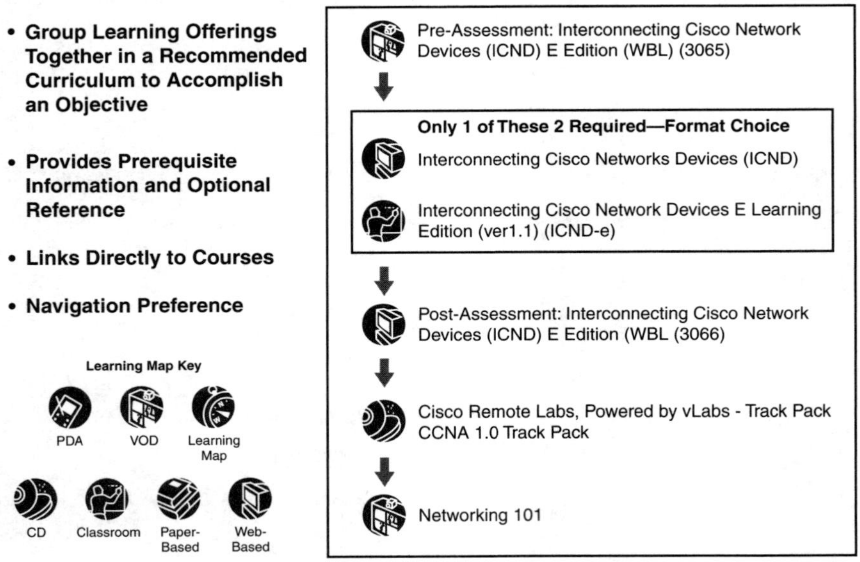

- **Group Learning Offerings Together in a Recommended Curriculum to Accomplish an Objective**

- **Provides Prerequisite Information and Optional Reference**

- **Links Directly to Courses**

- **Navigation Preference**

Learning Map Key: PDA, VOD, Learning Map, CD, Classroom, Paper-Based, Web-Based

Pre-Assessment: Interconnecting Cisco Network Devices (ICND) E Edition (WBL) (3065)

Only 1 of These 2 Required—Format Choice
Interconnecting Cisco Networks Devices (ICND)
Interconnecting Cisco Network Devices E Learning Edition (ver1.1) (ICND-e)

Post-Assessment: Interconnecting Cisco Network Devices (ICND) E Edition (WBL) (3066)

Cisco Remote Labs, Powered by vLabs - Track Pack CCNA 1.0 Track Pack

Networking 101

- Online remote lab programs that enable learners to connect to real networking equipment in a lab and receive instructional directions.

- Robust reporting capabilities under a tool called *MyLearning,* which enables individuals to track and monitor their curriculum progress, understand exactly which of their employees have taken and passed the assessment tests, and assess employee baseline product knowledge and progress. The tool also enables individuals to communicate their progress to their management.

- Electronic access to Cisco sponsored experts or "e-mentors," who can respond via e-mail, phone, or online (meeting learners in a lab, connecting to their screen, and walking them through an exercise).

- Online registration and a web catalog of classroom and virtual leader-led sessions offered across the globe, as well as searchable documents and presentations.

Through these tools, among others, PEC offered a robust capability for just-in-time personalized learning for employees across the extended enterprise of Cisco. With its online tests, availability of learning offerings, and quick access to product information through search tools, PEC became a working model of the productivity pyramid metaphor.

Feedback About PEC

The partners took some time to overcome initial barriers to PEC adoption. Like many innovations, early partner organizations experimented with PEC. Some of their earlier feedback that restricted rapid acceptance included the following:

- Lack of awareness about available content
- Slow access speeds over some Internet connections
- Preference for classroom training
- Desire for local languages
- High price of some content

As the program matured and continued to offer a wider range of tools and services, the objections about lack of specific content were resolved, and the program feedback is now incredibly positive. Over the years, PEC has become the most favored form of learning among partners. Learners report that this site fulfills more than 30 percent of their content needs. Approximately one fifth of learners in partner organizations report receiving half of their on-the-job training and information from PEC. (See Figure 8-3.)

Figure 8-3 *Preference for E-Learning*

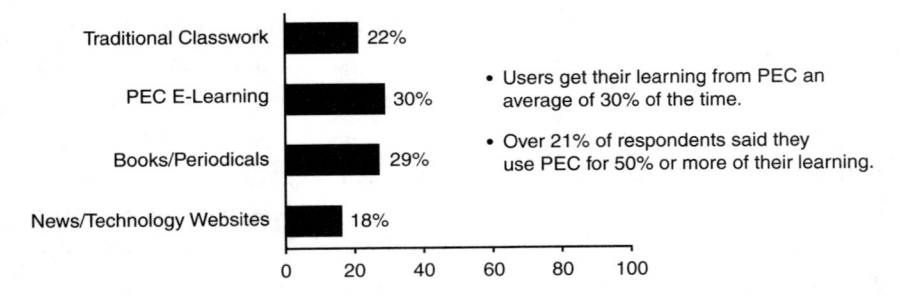

Partners use the PEC more than other modes to get their Cisco learning.

Source	Percentage
Traditional Classwork	22%
PEC E-Learning	30%
Books/Periodicals	29%
News/Technology Websites	18%

- Users get their learning from PEC an average of 30% of the time.
- Over 21% of respondents said they use PEC for 50% or more of their learning.

When asked to comment on how PEC has impacted their business, Cisco partners have mentioned the following:

- Helps sell or recommend Cisco products and services
- Serves as primary source of Cisco training
- Lowers cost of doing business
- Reduces time to knowledge
- Increases confidence with customers
- Helps stay current
- Differentiates Cisco from other vendors

As of July 2004, the total number of subscribers exceeded 160,000. More than 25,000 companies spread out among 132 countries were using the site. About a dozen local-language courses were available. More than 500 new users were signing up for the program each week. Internet learning has now turned channel communication (to and with) into a strategic advantage by improving partner success and loyalty. The numbers alone demonstrate the widespread adoption of the PEC.

Chapter 8: Productivity in the Extended Enterprise

Business Benefits of PEC

As a result of the efforts, sales force and support readiness among partners is now more efficient, timelier, and more relevant to a constantly changing environment. Partner organizations report benefits such as savings in training expenses, increased productivity, and increased customer satisfaction. According to one estimate, use of PEC saves partner organizations 11 hours per month per employee. (See Figure 8-4.)

Figure 8-4   *PEC Business Impact*

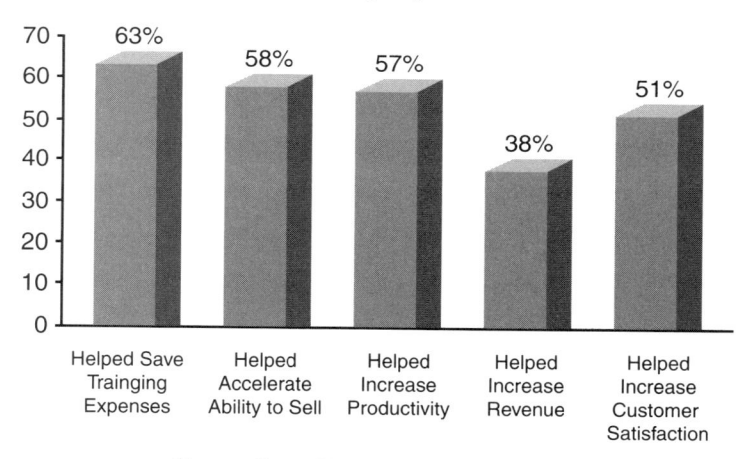

The PEC has helped Cisco Partners increase their revenue, productivity and cost savings by between 38% and 63%.

- Helped Save Trainging Expenses: 63%
- Helped Accelerate Ability to Sell: 58%
- Helped Increase Productivity: 57%
- Helped Increase Revenue: 38%
- Helped Increase Customer Satisfaction: 51%

Hours Saved Per Month   11
132 Hours Annual Productivity Increase Per Person

Not only does the portal enable learners to access content at will, but it also saves the Cisco sales force the time it used to spend training partners on the road. That role has now been assumed by PEC, which offers the sales force the time to focus on customer needs rather than training.

According to Cisco estimates, PEC helped generate $41 million in savings for the company in fiscal year 2003. Of that $41 million in savings, almost 20 percent was from time efficiencies, and the other 80 percent was through cost reduction (for example, reduced cost of labs, travel, lodging). (See Table 8-1.)

(103)

Table 8-1 *FY 2003 E-Learning Cisco Benefits*

Internet Business Solutions	Cost Avoidance	Time Efficiencies	Internet Capabilities Benefit
Sales – Systems Engineers	$23M	$28M	$51M
Partners	$32M	$9M	$41M
Customer Advocacy	$7M	$13M	$20M
Engineering	$4M	$6M	$10M
Manufacturing/ HR/IT	$8M	$12M	$20M
Total			$142M

Source: Cisco IBSG, Internet Capabilities Analysis, Fiscal Year 2003

Using the tool has helped partner organizations achieve the criteria of increased certified individuals, increased partner specializations, and improved penetration of product and technology updates in the channel. Evidence of the success is demonstrated in the partner satisfaction ratings, as shown in Figure 8-5.

Figure 8-5 *Customer Satisfaction Grew with the Introduction in March 2000 of the PEC Tool*

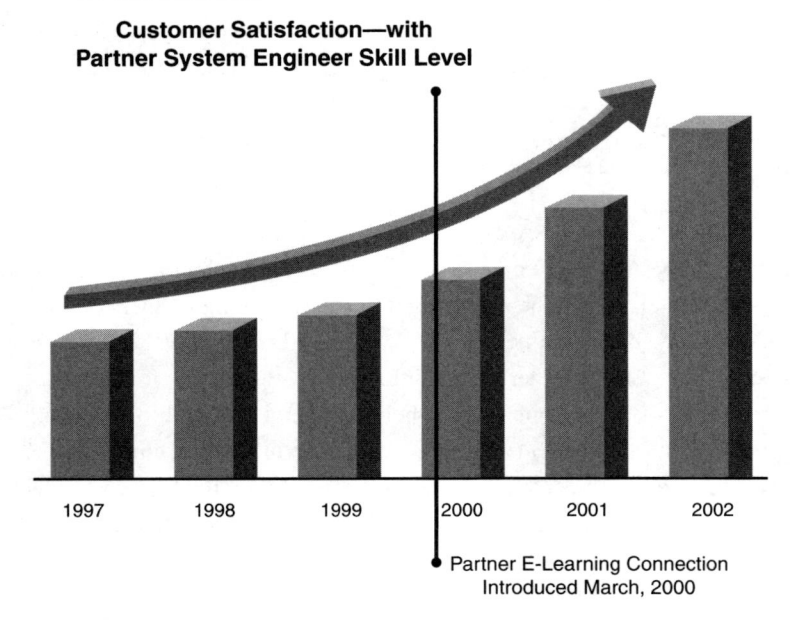

With compelling business benefits, the value of the e-learning portal has been apparent to Cisco resellers. Reseller employees continue to benefit from the learning tools, in turn offering productivity advantages to their employers, customers, and Cisco.

Recommendations for Building an Extended Enterprise

The leap to create an external-facing e-learning effort from an internal effort might not be as traumatic as some might perceive at first. The Cisco experience presented some insights into external Internet learning efforts:

- Start now and improve as you go.

  Business imperatives, rather than development soundness, should determine time to market. If a business problem can be solved through a solution that offers limited features, bring it to market and let the early adopters run with it. Improvements and additions can always be made in response to customer feedback.

- Leverage industry expertise (partner for partners).

  If speed to market is a key consideration for creating a reseller learning network, outsourcing components of an Internet learning infrastructure is a valuable strategy. It avoids the pitfalls of reinventing the wheel and reduces administrative pressures on planners.

- Focus on relevant and timely content.

  The 80-20 principle works for content selection as well. Planners should deliver content that has a wider audience appeal and should offer resellers anytime-anywhere customer access. Focus first on easy wins with impact.

- Marketing *and* IT are key.

  Coordinating with IT on the development front, even with an outsourced solution, is critical to success. Only through coordination with IT can possible integration issues be identified early in the process. When creating tools for the reseller or partner channel, marketing will eventually bring the solution to market. Sound program management will ensure that both stakeholders are on any task force or team that gets pulled together.

- Drive solutions from the user perspective, not from available IT tools.

   Obvious as it may sound, many e-learning projects become a victim of a technology-centric thinking instead of focusing on user needs. Leveraging excess IT capacity for Internet learning is a tempting proposition; however, if the tools and the infrastructure do not offer the flexibility for realizing customer success, the project may be at risk of failing right from the start.

- Evaluate the funding and resource model.

   The business model behind a program should be robust. A sound business proposition is easier to sell to senior management for funding. Besides upfront investment in the program, recurring expenses and cash-flow requirements should be identified.

- Measure and track relevant metrics.

   Customer success proven through business metrics carries weight within and outside of the organization. Without empirical evidence of success, continued support for the project becomes subject to the vagaries of discretionary budgets.

- Balance innovation and standardization.

   Although innovative solutions help to create a buzz around an application, reaching learners should be the primary motivation behind such innovation. Planners should first ensure that quality instruction and communication is enabled at the last mile for the maximum number of learners.

- Create virtual project teams from the beginning...and keep them engaged.

   Cross-functional collaboration ensures necessary alignment with organizations, such as channel development, human resources, training, marketing, finance, and IT. Ensuring sustained representation and input on the project through a virtual team or task force enables organizational buy-in into decisions.

- Involve executive stakeholders.

  Executive support and sponsorship is necessary for global adoption of an external learning program that impacts learners across theaters, regions, and channels. Project planners and managers should keep executives tuned to the project outcomes, progress, and impact on revenue.

Conclusion

The success with PEC among reseller organizations clearly demonstrates the need to look at e-learning initiatives as part of management, marketing, and training functions, not just conversion of content into technology media. Creation of a quality program remains the primary objective in all such initiatives; however, responsiveness to customer needs and a focus on productivity advantages for the users will help to ensure the desired adoption among learners.

CHAPTER 9

PICKING A NETWORKING DREAM TEAM

Key Take-Away

Besides e-communication and e-training, assessments help identify talent that contributes toward productivity advantages. The merger efforts at Equant bore fruit because the technological alignment was made possible by a group of certified individuals.

A key component of an integrated learning model is assessment. How can management determine who has acquired the skill sets and who has not? How do they decide how to reward individuals based on their skills? Proctored exams and certifications offer tools to ensure that the most qualified and talented knowledge workers within an organization are identified and recognized. Research indicates that employers that have certified talent on staff are more productive than those without. (See Figure 9-1.)

Figure 9-1 The Productivity Advantage of Certified Staff[1]

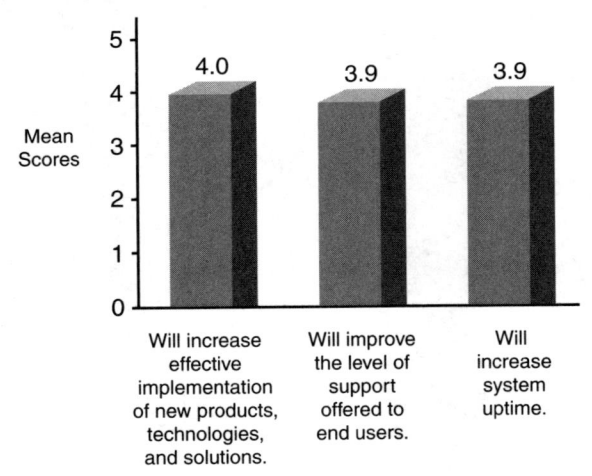

Mean Scores:
- Will increase effective implementation of new products, technologies, and solutions: 4.0
- Will improve the level of support offered to end users: 3.9
- Will increase system uptime: 3.9

According to a 2002 industry data from International Data Corporation (IDC) on certifications, IT managers and buyers associate a high level of credibility with certifications.[2] Employers and customers perceive certified employees as "worth the investment" it takes to prepare those individuals.

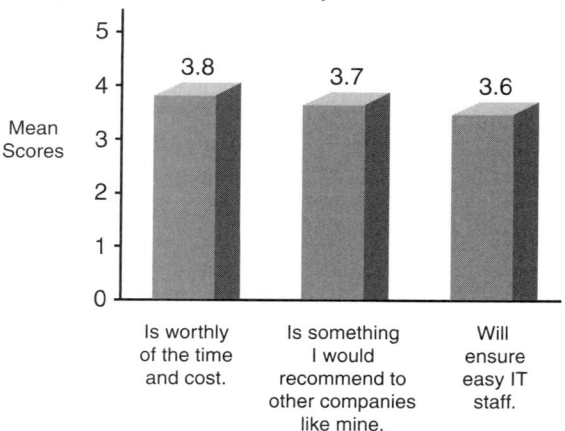

Figure 9-2 *Certifications Build Credibility*

[Bar chart — Mean Scores:
- Is worthly of the time and cost: 3.8
- Is something I would recommend to other companies like mine: 3.7
- Will ensure easy IT staff: 3.6]

The tendency for employers to consider certified talent as individuals who might leave the organization for better job prospects appears to be a thing of the past. Employers encourage certifications to generate skill and versatility among employees and to foster employee loyalty through a commitment to lifelong learning.[3] Figure 9-3 shows the top three value propositions certifications provide to employees.

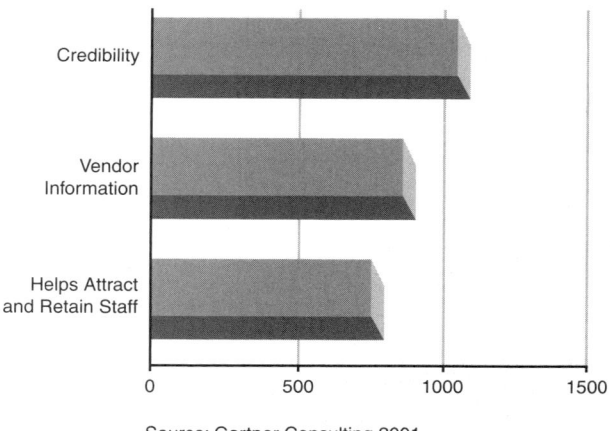

Figure 9-3 *Certifications Help Retention*

[Horizontal bar chart:
- Credibility: ~1100
- Vendor Information: ~900
- Helps Attract and Retain Staff: ~750]

Source: Gartner Consulting 2001

The Equant case study discusses the strategic value of having certified talent on staff.

Integration Challenge at Equant

Today, Equant is an industry leader in global IP and data services for multinational businesses, providing worldwide IP virtual private network (VPN) services to corporate customers. A market leader with thousands of large business customers—including some of the world's Top 100 companies—Equant emerged after a merger between two parent companies in June 2001: Global One and Sita/Equant.

A merger of Sita/Equant and Global One was slated to deliver significant cost savings and synergies. Operating cost savings were expected at more than $300 million per year. After the merger, the combined company was envisioned to operate one of the world's largest seamless data networks, connecting key business centers in 220 countries and territories worldwide, with local support in 145 countries in English and 40 other languages. Sita/Equant's extensive network, connecting key business centers in more than 220 countries and territories, also proved an ideal fit with the denser 70-country Global One worldwide network. The strong national coverage by Global One in several countries brought access points closer to Sita/Equant customers.

If the international networks of the two telecommunications companies, Global One and Sita/Equant, could be integrated, the economies of scale, reduction of duplicate costs, and the pooling of revenue would offer tremendous gains to the emerging company. However, merging two networks with "lives" of their own is easier said than done. To reap the productivity advantages of the merger, the new company (Equant) had to find a way to converge two legacy networks into one.

Merger Relied on Talent

The cost savings and the synergy of a combined network hinged on successful integration. The savings had to be realized within two years after the merger. Because the former Equant and Global One networks were based on a combination of Nortel and Cisco technologies meant that the integration had to be accomplished by engineers who were well versed with not only Cisco solutions, but also with IP technologies.

Chapter 9: Picking a Networking Dream Team

The engineers needed to ensure that the diverse and disparate networks acted as one. The features of each network were not only to be preserved, but also delivered across the new, combined network. With the fate of the merger depending on successful integration, Equant needed qualified engineers who could demonstrate credentials that were necessary for bringing about the integration and ensuring that the project did not experience cost and time overruns.

Certified Talent Delivers Results

Before the merger opportunity, both Equant and Global One had traditionally relied on Cisco certifications to ensure that the networking staff kept current with IP skills. As a result of its commitment to credentials and certifications, Equant boasted a pool of Cisco-certified individuals with designations such as CCIEs, CCNPs, and CCNAs.

Because of Equant's and Global One's past comfort level with Cisco-certified engineers, the IP talent needed to integrate the two networks was picked from a pool of Cisco-certified network engineers.

"A world-class IP portfolio needs world-class support," said Per Johanson, group manager for Equant. "Time to market is a key determinant for business success, and having a diverse and talented team of Cisco-certified individuals on a project ensured that the integration would be on time and trouble free. Cisco certifications offered a means to identify the talented and motivated engineers among the pool of networking staff we have."

The final integration of the two networks came two months ahead of schedule and coincided with the one-year anniversary of the transaction in which Equant and Global One merged. Hailed by Didier Delepine, President and CEO of Equant as "one of the first in the telecommunications industry that has really worked," unification of the two networks was expected to generate more than 50 percent of the annualized operating-cost savings.

Benefits to Equant

Transmission and site costs dropped substantially as the two networks became one, and the total number of network sites was reduced. By the end of 2002, 70 redundant network sites were closed.

Duplicate capital spending reduced by approximately $75 million per year. The new company realized network costs savings by rationalizing and restructuring the transmission infrastructure of Equant and Global One and by pooling resources for network planning, engineering, and operations. Productivity gains also resulted from the integration of staff functions and systems and the streamlining of the entire organization.

Conclusion

The Equant experience demonstrates the value of investing in certification of knowledge workers. Confidence that your staff can deliver results when dealing with unfamiliar projects is possible only if they have been thoroughly tested on a range of scenarios through robust assessment or certification exams. More than mere skills, having a certification demonstrates a willingness to learn on the part of the worker.

For a strategic merger to yield the desired results, Equant relied on its core of certified engineers to enable a technology-integration project. With the goal of doing more with less, a committed and qualified core of project staff can play a strategic role in an organization's success.

Endnotes

[1] The Relationship Between Certifications and Partnership Programs, IDC328374, Cushing Anderson and Steve McHale, December 2002.

[2] ibid.

[3] Gartner Study on Certifications and Training 2001.

CHAPTER 10

CERTIFICATIONS AS A BRANDING TOOL: SPONSORING A CERTIFICATION PROGRAM

> **Key Take-Away**
>
> Sponsoring a certification program has more to do with a business strategy than with learning content. Learning content can be offered through training or communication tools, but creating a certification program is more about meeting a brand or support commitment to customers than it is about developing an exam that validates knowledge.

The most common use of certifications involves individuals completing association or vendor-based certifications to demonstrate their skills to employers or customers. Vendor-based certifications are those sponsored by manufacturers such as Cisco Systems. Association certifications, also referred to as neutral certifications, are offered by a consortium of corporations or a nonprofit organization representing an industry. From an organizational point of view, relying on existing certification programs to validate employee or reseller skills is a cost-effective approach to assessment. For organizations that rely heavily on the skill sets of their distribution channel for the success of their products or services, however, sponsoring certifications to qualify competent individuals in a reseller or a partner network might be a worthwhile investment.

Sponsoring a certification can serve as a feasible customer benefit that can help to enhance the corporate brand of the sponsoring organization. A corporate brand is often described as consistent customer experience with a product or a service. A certification program ensures a common body of knowledge among those individuals who support customer purchases with installation and troubleshooting. Certifications ensure that a common body of knowledge and skill sets across a range of diverse customer support individuals helps to meet customer expectations of a consistent post-sale experience.

Sponsoring a certification might involve creating exams that assess an individual's proficiency with skills. A manufacturer relying on a reseller network to service or support might choose to link discount rates or benefits to skills development. Certifications can play a role in validating which of the resellers or partners have acquired the necessary skills to service or support the product.

Certifications offer the sponsoring organization the confidence that
- Customer leads and requests will be well managed.
- Partners or resellers have made a commitment of skills and talent.
- Best practices are permeating through the reseller network.

For the partners or resellers, certifications are valuable because those demonstrate

- Commitment to current and potential customers
- Advantage over competition
- Expertise in deploying, delivering, or supporting the sponsoring organization

A review of the Cisco Partner Program certification offers a perspective into planning and defining a certification program to strengthen the reseller channel. The following case explains the program briefly and highlights the most important features.

Certifying Partners or Resellers at Cisco

Partners who resell and deploy Cisco hardware and solutions follow a stringent set of guidelines from Cisco to maintain their value proposition. The Cisco Partner Program affords organizations strength in the marketplace through technology learning, specialization, best practices, and credibility. The Cisco Partner Program provides a level playing field so that value-add partners are not at a disadvantage to pure hardware resellers. The company also consistently evaluates its partner requirements to ensure that they support sustainable business models. Partner status in the Cisco environment is based on meeting certain criteria.

Based on an evaluation of their strengths, Cisco assigns the partner organization Gold, Silver, or Premier status. The distinction between each of the tiers is based on the level of support and human resources dedicated to supporting Cisco solutions. So a reseller who makes a larger commitment in terms of people and resources to supporting and selling Cisco gear would be entitled to a higher tier and, as a result, preferred discount rates. Table 10-1 details the differences in each level of partner certification.

Table 10-1   *Requirements Summary*

Career Certified Individuals			
	Gold	Silver	Premier
Sales Experts (CSE)	4	2	1
Associates (CCNA, CCDA)	4	2	2
Professionals (CCNP, CCDP, CCIP, CCSP)	4	2	0
Experts (CCIEs)	4	2	0
Minimum # of Individuals	16	8	3
one additional CCIE for each $40 million in annual Cisco revenue			
Point Requirements			
	Gold	Silver	Premier
Specialization Points	70	40	20
Extra Credit Points	30	20	0
Total Points	**100**	**60**	**20**

- Career certified individuals

  Cisco offers career certifications at the Associate, Professional, and Expert levels to validate skills among networking professionals and to help companies identify networking talent for recruitment. Having Cisco-certified individuals on staff adds value to a partner organization when customers consider organizational competence to deploy networking solutions.

- Support requirements

  Support requirements measure an organization's ability to respond to customer support needs. Partners demonstrate strength of factors such as call center support, availability of technical assistance, response time to customer call, and management oversight under this criterion.

- Customer satisfaction

  Partners are expected to meet or exceed regional targets for average customer satisfaction scores on a rating scale of 1 to 5.

- Specialization points

  The Cisco Partner Specialization Program allows Cisco partners to develop and demonstrate their expertise in technologies, solutions, and services through structured training road maps and a knowledge-validation process. With increased emphasis in the networking marketplace on specific technology areas such as content networking, security, wireless, and IP telephony, Cisco often encourages partners to pursue specific skills in those areas beyond the general skills. The expertise enables an organization to differentiate itself from competitors, pursue new markets, and migrate to higher-margin, services-based and solutions-based business models. Partners receive points for completing a specialization toward their status.

- **Extra credit** (by exceeding the previous metrics)

   The extra credit points needed to achieve Silver or Gold certification can be earned by having additional specializations, extra career-certified individuals above and beyond those required in the base requirements, or by exceeding the customer satisfaction target for the region. This component of the program allows an organization to gain either more specialization or technical expertise, or to be rewarded for providing higher levels of customer satisfaction. Table 10-2 shows the point system.

Table 10-2   Specialization Points

Specialization	Points
IP Communications	40
Content Networking	30
IP Telephony Services	30
Cable	25
Universal Dial Access	25
VPN/Security	25
VPN/Security Services	25
IP Communications Express	20
Network Management	20
Public Access	20
Routing and Switching	20
Wireless LAN	20
Global Commerce	20

Creating a Certification Program

Knowing that certifications can be a strong marketing tool for partner development and customer satisfaction, many decision makers tend to believe that certifications can somehow bolster their product image and generate sales. This assumption is often misleading. If a decision maker views certifications as a sales tool and increasing the number of certified individuals as a means of increasing adoption of product, the probability of failure might be high. Experience has shown that launching a certification program does not by itself generate demand for the products and services around which the content for the certification exams and training have been created. In essence, the sponsoring organization should view certifications as a customer support tool that enhances the organization's credibility or corporate brand to retain customers rather than viewing it as a promotional tool to acquire new customers.

On the other hand, if certifications are viewed as a means of improving customer experience and satisfaction with the product, the approach may well be worth the investment because it can help tremendously with improving customer loyalty and retaining existing customers (that is, discouraging them from switching to a competitor's brand). Although subtle, the distinction can remarkably alter the focus of the program for the sponsoring organizations. An organization that views customer experience and customer satisfaction as a criterion for success for a certification program is less likely to lower the bar on exam integrity to speed up completions. Similarly, organizational metrics to justify and evaluate the program will differ.

Following are key questions to consider when determining whether a certification program should be launched:

- How do we ensure quality when supporting or servicing customers?
- How can a qualified pool of talent be best created to support or service our products?
- Will training suffice, or is a certification program imperative?
- To what extent are certifications likely to affect customer experience and satisfaction?
- To what extent are the partners or resellers likely to adopt the certifications?
- Can certifications be replaced with online assessments?

- Do we have the distinction and detail in content that existing neutral certifications available from associations do not address?
- Do the desired metrics justify an investment?

Answers to these questions are likely to indicate whether there is a need for sponsoring a certification program. If after reviewing the situation, planners determine that it does, a decision to move forward can be executed.

Developing a Certification Program

Before launching a certification program, the sponsoring organization should define the skill sets and proficiency levels that the certification will validate. The development effort should include four phases:

1. Business analysis

    To ensure that the program meets the needs of customers, a sponsoring organization should conduct a business analysis to assess the demand and identify the benefits of the program. Defining the productivity impact of a certification program on customer satisfaction and partner performance should be the cornerstone of the analysis. The business analysis should include the following components:

    a. Internal analysis

        An internal analysis should cover the strategic considerations behind pursuing a certification program. The strategic advantages might be in the form of distribution benefits or customer franchise for the sponsoring organization, but identifying those should be the first step in any internal analysis. Similarly, available resources, cost of developing a program, availability of subject matter or domain experts, and needs expressed by the stakeholders should be considered.

        The internal analysis should specify a few options of how a program might accomplish the strategic advantages sought and what might be the objectives. The analyses also include an effort to narrow down the subject matter or domain to be covered through the certification based on input from in-house experts or stakeholders.

b. Candidate profile

Program planners should invest in understanding the needs of potential candidates, their demographic and psychographic profiles, and their learning styles and preferences. A certification program should be launched only if planners can demonstrate that the proposed benefits will meet the candidates' specific needs. A program with a strong rationale and evidence of success should not be taken at face value unless the proposition is borne out through market research of the target audience.

c. Market analysis

A certification program should emphasize content area, subject matter, or domains that exhibit a growth pattern. Identifying expanding domain or content areas becomes necessary because certification programs need a sustainable exam volume to break even. Emerging industries or markets represent viable opportunities to target for training and certification opportunities. Experience has shown that demand for certification often lags a year or so behind the market demand for products or services in the targeted domain area.

When projecting exam volume and exam pricing to assess revenue from a certification program, existing or potential competitive entries from other vendors or associations should be accounted for. If the volume does not seem sustainable through a certification offered by a single organization, collaboration among vendors representing a common industry should be considered.

d. Job task analysis

When determining the content, it often helps to focus on underlying principles behind a product rather than specific product-based certifications. Because the product life cycle is shorter than that of an underlying technology or discipline, a broader approach to content and assessment development might make the program more appealing for the candidate.

By definition, a job task analysis (JTA) reviews and determines the skills needed to successfully perform on the job. The JTA addresses

Chapter 10: Certifications as a Branding Tool

specific skill sets to be assessed and determines the weight that the industry assigns to each tasks and skill for the particular job. Through the analysis, developers can determine which types of skills can be assessed through certification exams.

2. Program development

The program development phase essentially sets the ground for organizing the program design, business plan, assessment tools, and a strategy for learning support. The critical components of a program development phase should include the following steps:

a. Business plan

Based on the business analysis, a business plan for the certification program should be created. At the very least, the business plan should attempt to answer the following five questions:

- What is the program's business value to the organization?
- Do the tangible and intangible benefits of the program exceed the cost of developing and supporting it?
- How will the program be positioned to customers and partners?
- What kind of a marketing effort or plan will be pursued to make the program a success with customers?
- What kind of organizational support will be needed to manage the program?

The business plan should form the basis of support within the organization for such an undertaking. The business plan should help to directly answer questions raised by senior management about the value or justification behind the program. The business plan should also allow an organization to determine how to proceed and how much to allocate toward the program. (For additional details, see Chapter 7, "Targeted Learning: Are You *Indeed* Ready?")

b. Program design

The program design defines the number of certification tracks and levels that might be offered. For each certification, the program design also addresses the number of exams that the candidates might be required to pass. The program should also define what prerequisite knowledge candidates must possess ahead of pursuing a certification.

And finally, the program design should specify how the certifications align or articulate with other certifications offered by the organization or industry.

c. Creation of assessment tools

Based on the findings from the JTA, exam developers can develop the blueprint for an exam. Written by subject matter experts, the exam questions are validated by psychometricians (question item experts) to determine whether the questions are indeed deriving what they are intended to find out about the candidates' skills.

The exams are run in beta to determine passing scores. Passing scores are determined only after exam developers have the confidence that the question items and the exam forms are reflective of candidate skills.

d. Learning support

Within the context of the productivity pyramid metaphor, it stands to reason that any certification launched should be based on some form of available training or knowledge content. However, availability of such content might not precede the development of a certification program. Organizations creating assessments without existing training in place should ensure that, at minimum, the necessary learning support materials are offered as white papers, articles, guides, and manuals prior to launching a certification.

To generate trial and interest, candidates need support when preparing for the exams. Experience shows that candidates often prefer to follow a defined road map when preparing to pass a certification. That type of learning support can often be delivered through a formal curriculum defined and delivered by the sponsoring organization or its authorized providers. Learning support can also emerge through informal road maps created with the help of manuals, books, and workshops. Either way, for a certification to have success among customers, a strategy for learning support should be addressed while defining program parameters and design.

Chapter 10: Certifications as a Branding Tool

3 Program implementation

The program implementation identifies specific considerations for making the program available in the certification marketplace. Some of the considerations include the following:

a. Marketing launch and customer communications

A successful program launch should describe the certification program requirements and benefits to candidates through an integrated marketing communications. Through websites, frequently asked questions, press releases, and customer service centers, an organization can foster an understanding about the program and its scope in the minds of potential candidates.

Potential candidates are most likely to follow up with a range of "what-if" scenarios to assess the potential investment and return for them. Therefore, some form of two-way communications should be enabled through the course of the program, and especially in early days of the launch, to allow probing questions and queries from customers. Continual market analyses and evaluation surveys are some of the ways of assessing two-way communication.

b. Testing channel delivery

Test delivery is often outsourced to delivery partners with testing sites located worldwide. Choosing a recognized delivery partner is the first step to ensuring that exam integrity and customer satisfaction are not compromised. Exam security and integrity can be severely affected if exam delivery parameters and requirements are not defined. Readiness at the testing channel sites is essential to a smooth program rollout.

c. Delivering road map for test preparation

Having the learning road maps in place has a significant impact on certification adoption. In partnership with authorized training providers and publishers, the sponsoring organization should ensure availability of courseware, practice, or preparation materials for candidates to use. For low-volume certifications, e-training and e-communication can help deliver preparation materials cost-effectively to a dispersed audience.

4 Program management

The program management component of certifications should ensure that the business value and assessment integrity remain intact for the program. Through ongoing evaluation of market needs and continual program updates, a sponsoring organization can ensure that the program remains relevant over the long run. The program management function also ensures that the program continually evolves to stay current with the candidate, content, and organization needs.

Some program management components include the following:

a. Maintenance

Candidate results from the exams delivered under a certification program should be tracked and monitored to ensure that candidates are accurately credited for their achievements. The program should maintain a database of certified individuals that provides candidates with access to only their own records. After candidates complete the requirements, the program administration should ensure that they receive all the appropriate recognition, such as completion certificates, program logos, access privileges, price discounts, or preferred support.

Program maintenance should also include review of performance on exam questions to ensure that the questions are updated and revised frequently to keep pace with changes in the marketplace. A program that continually updates itself in response to the market, job, or skill needs reduces the risk of assessing candidates on obsolete content and also discourages candidates from assuming a "studying-for-the-test" approach to certifications. Ongoing job task analyses, periodic surveys, and focus groups help validate the relevance of the program to the workforce.

b. Customer relationship management

Besides providing customers with access to a resource for answering and responding to questions about the program, customer relationship management includes access to support or knowledge tools for those who meet program requirements and certify. When a candidate invests in a program, the individual makes a commitment to the

Chapter 10: Certifications as a Branding Tool

sponsoring organization as much as he does to the certification. If a sponsoring organization views the candidate who certifies as a loyal customer, affinity programs to strengthen the loyalty will yield benefits in generating advocates within the customer base.

Creation of a community of practice around the topics of interest for certified individuals offers an opportunity for knowledge sharing. Tools such as discussion groups, chat rooms, and peer reviews can be enabled for such a community of practice. Additional information items, such as program updates, certification-related news, learning games, and salary surveys can also be offered as a bundle of benefits to certified individuals.

c. Marketing

The value and the integrity of the program should be demonstrated not only to potential candidates, but also to those employers who hire those candidates. Employers or customers who seek certain skill sets view a certification as a screening tool for employment if they determine that the program is credible. Program administrators should ensure that the marketing message describing the value of the program is presented to potential employers.

d. Evaluation

Program administrators should periodically demonstrate the productivity impact of a certification program on the partner or customer constituents. At the very minimum, through anecdotal evidence and, preferably, through formal research, the progress toward program goals, employer satisfaction, and individual (or candidate) interest should be measured for effectiveness. Such data provides valuable input for senior management and useful insights for program direction and decision making.

A few data points for assessing whether a certification program is having the desired impact are as follows:

- Measure the self-reported intent to purchase or purchase again (loyalty) through surveys to determine whether customers with certifications respond more favorably than those without one.

- Assess the support calls received by the help desk to determine whether the frequency of complaints received from certified customers are lower than those raised by noncertified customers.
- Compare the level of satisfaction ratings garnered by pre- and post-sales teams with certified individuals versus those without certified team members.

Conclusion

As highlighted in the four steps of business analysis, program development, program implementation, and program management, a certifications initiative should be viewed as a customer support or loyalty program within an organization. Although the responsibility for managing such a program might lie with the learning leaders within an organization, the eventual success of it rests with sales and distribution groups, marketing, technical support, and customer relationship management. Certifications are an organizational or corporate commitment, not merely a departmental function.

Endnote

For the writing of this chapter, the authors thank Galton-Prometric for its support and assistance with information about the certifications development process.

CHAPTER 11

THE BUILDING BLOCKS

> ### *Key Take-Away*
> A review of the building blocks during the planning phases helps an organization avoid pitfalls during an e-learning implementation.

When developing a learning strategy within an organization, planners should deploy specific components to make an integrated learning effort a success. Ensuring that all the pieces integrate well and work in unison is easier said than done. Even though the pieces might not appear to fit at first, proactive planning and stakeholder buy-in will ensure that, as time passes, the pieces converge to present a process that is robust and, more importantly, effective.

Successful implementation relies as much on the organization's management skills as it does on picking the relevant components. The next two chapters address specific implementation steps.

Begin with Knowledge-Sharing Tools: E-Communications

Moving forward with an integrated learning effort should begin with the deployment of knowledge-sharing tools. Knowledge sharing is actually just e-communication: the tools that make it possible to get information from one person to many people quickly and consistently. Because of its widespread user access, knowledge sharing is likely to most conspicuously impact the organization. Because knowledge sharing does not replace any instructor-led training efforts, the resistance is likely to be the least. Knowledge sharing will likely have productivity advantages, affect a maximum number of participants, and save travel dollars for the organization. Even the most skeptical of stakeholders has a hard time arguing against the benefits of and savings from deploying an e-communication suite.

The Field E-Learning Connection (FELC) case discussed in Chapter 3, "E-Learning Under the Microscope," is an example of how white papers, product documents, product updates through video presentations, and news items were placed on the portal first to engage the internal sales force. Only after the e-communication component took off was e-training added as a component to the portal.

Functional Integration

In most organizations, voice, video, and data systems are managed by separate organizations. Most likely, a telecom department addresses voice needs, a production or media department deals with video needs, and an information technology unit manages all the data systems. Deployment of an integrated IP network allows an organization to deliver its video, voice, and data over a single platform. Although such migration is likely to facilitate functional integration alone, a successful e-communication effort does not depend on functional integration. For an e-communication effort to succeed, user needs should be championed by those responsible for learning and business objectives, while those responsible for technology should address those learning and business needs with viable technology solutions.

Partner E-Learning Connection (PEC), discussed in Chapter 8, "Productivity in the Extended Enterprise: Internet Learning Offers a Competitive Edge with Channel Partners," is an example of how the needs of the Cisco reseller base drove the development of an online learning portal. Although the development and maintenance of the portal involves significant participation from the IT team within Cisco, the Worldwide Channels organization inside of Cisco champions learner needs through content leadership.

Cross-Functional Management

Cross-functional collaboration—that is, cooperation across departments responsible for relevant voice, video, and data components—should be coupled with a dotted-line reporting structure to the lead e-communication deployment organization. Business leadership for cross-functional collaboration of video, voice, and data does not reside in the same place in every organization. It is driven by strategic intent and the enterprise's necessity.

Cross-functional collaboration between IT and the Channels organization on PEC offers opportunities for continuous improvement of the learning portal through the creation of enhanced learning features and evaluation tools.

Technical Tools and Capabilities

Deployment of portals, video, and search functionality means user-friendly access to e-communication. For example, management can use video for policy updates, product updates, or executive announcements.

Portals offer a thematic selection of content relevant to a subject matter, topic, or learner group. Portals provide users easy access to content that is organized and managed thematically. Video and other presentation tools enable learners to access content anytime-anywhere across an organization. If content is available, learners should be able to find and retrieve that content through robust search tools.

In the case of PEC, the ease of access to product updates and presentations via the portals is evident among employees in reseller organizations. When employees in these reseller organizations face a certification or exam deadline, the PEC serves a source of learning content for anytime-anyplace access.

Content Life Cycle Management

Besides creating high-demand content, organizations must maintain a current content library or a single logical repository to keep up with the fast-changing needs of the learners. With content being a key cost consideration in the development of learning tools, a balance between content life cycle and reuse must be established. Determining which content items are to be kept for use later and which can be discarded can be done effectively only if such decisions are based on policy, practice, and workflow. Reusable objects and tools allow existing content to be repurposed, thereby reducing the cost of curriculum development.

For portals such as FELC and PEC at Cisco, the availability of certain products, emphasis on specific technologies, and alignment with certification exam curriculum offer useful guidelines when determining the relevance of content. Those content items with potential learning applications are archived, whereas those that appear to offer no potential learning value are removed from the database altogether.

Distributed Authoring

Distributed authoring refers to the ability within an organization to tap into the collective talent of many subject-matter experts to develop content. For e-learning to achieve widespread adoption across the organization, support distributed authoring. When subject-matter specialists located worldwide within an organization can contribute toward e-communication or e-training content through user-friendly content-authoring tools, content is generated more rapidly. If content contribution is widespread and user experience with the authoring process is satisfactory, these authors will also serve as champions of e-learning within the organization.

Product updates and policy updates at Cisco can be presented through video using an easy-to-use recording tool that runs off of an employee's PC. No matter how remote an employee, if there is a message that needs to reach the sales force or other major constituent within Cisco, the employee can use the video tool to get a 5- to 10-minute update on a portal through a video-on-demand (VoD) application.

Skills Gap Analysis

Understanding where the skill gaps are within a workforce allows for the creation of targeted learning plans. The hit-and-miss approach of training should be replaced with a more deliberate approach of pre-assessment that identifies learning needs. Instead of investing many hours in an instructor-led, face-to-face class (and many general knowledge and skills topics), an individual can review specific learning modules, read specific white papers, or pass select exams that are intended to meet his skills gaps. By pinpointing individual learning needs and following up with targeted learning plans, organizations increase the return on learning dollars invested.

The MyDevelopment tool discussed in Chapter 7, "Targeted Learning: Are You *Indeed* Ready?," offers an example of how a curriculum and assessment path *can* be created around not just the learning style of an individual, but also the specific learning needs of that individual.

Learner Buy-In

Learner buy-in refers to the process of generating adoption within an organization. Achieving learner buy-in is a two-step process: identifying incentives for e-learning adoption and facilitating its use. Identifying incentives means demonstrating to line managers or supervisors that learning is indeed an essential business function and its adoption directly impacts departmental productivity through reduced cost, better time utilization, and improved revenue. Few line managers would shun an opportunity to reduce cost, improve utilization of their team, and improve revenue. When the line managers support e-learning, employees adopt it.

In Chapter 4, "BearingPoint Makes Grand Slam with Internet Learning—A Case Study," the discussion illustrates how the organization adopted e-learning wholesale to familiarize the entire work force with e-business. The potential productivity advantages from arming the employees with such knowledge offered a compelling incentive for the organization to commit resources to e-learning.

Facilitating use of e-learning includes ensuring that production and delivery factors address learner needs and circumstances. Video lectures available for downloaded for later viewing, that are accessible to those who connect over dial up, or that are accessible through a learner-friendly portal, might boost the adoption of e-learning.

Locus of Control

The adoption of e-learning in an organization should be the responsibility of business managers—not training or IT managers. This might be in operations, sales, or some other function that focuses on business problems and solutions. In certain cases, a cross-functional team—including operations, finance, training, and marketing—might be involved in the effort.

In any case, all participants must understand that deployment is a *business function*. In terms of business process improvement, the building blocks related to creating an e-learning effort are similar to those required for creating any new Internet business initiative. The skill demands on a team for deploying Internet learning in an organization are similar to those for any business process improvement. In essence, the champions of e-learning deployment should be familiar with change management.

The BearingPoint approach to e-learning engagement offers a useful illustration of the process. At BearingPoint, a program management office of professionals with expertise in a range of skills identifies needs and delivers solutions in the area of e-learning for the organization. The program office served as the change agent during the adoption phase of e-learning at BearingPoint.

> ### *Hindsight Is 20/20: Got It! What Next?*
>
> To start, you must have a general understanding of what needs to get done mixed with a dose of reality of what you can do.
>
> The first big step is to select a project. This is the most difficult part because picking a project represents the beginning of the action, visibility, and controversy that will be the hallmarks of your next 6 to 24 months.
>
> Initiating an e-learning project, if you've not yet taken that step, means you have to do something you might have little or no experience with, take some significant risks, be willing to explore the unknown at full speed, and generally be courageous in the face of known and unknown dangers.

One tool that can help you pick the project is the familiar quadrant chart. (See Figure 11-1.) Although the chart is somewhat intuitive, it suggests that it makes sense to pick a project that will be relatively easy to implement and that will also make a business impact. Easy might mean not complex, or might mean fast, or might perhaps mean cross-organizational teamwork is not required. The meaning of easy changes with each organization's variables. If you pick an easy project that has little or no visible business impact, you're not taking a big enough risk, and your success will be dismissed as an experiment that won't work in the real world.

Figure 11-1   *Selecting a Project—Risk/Performance Grid*

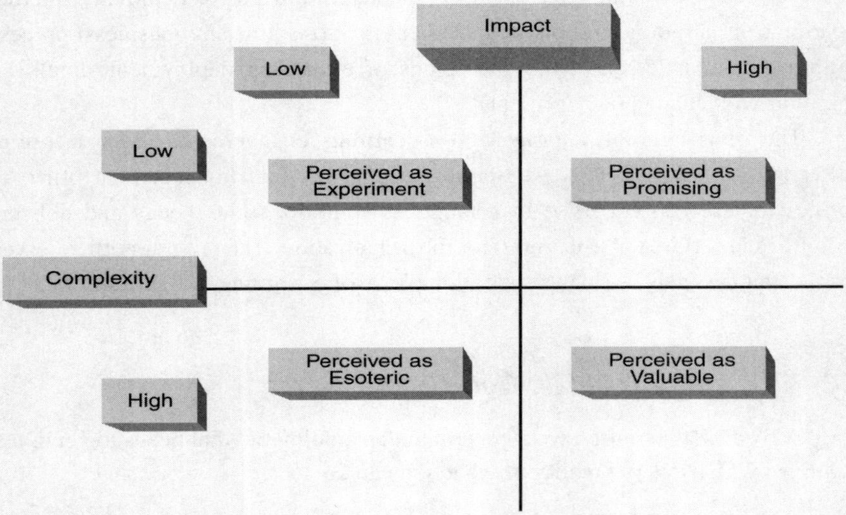

	Impact Low	Impact High
Complexity Low	Perceived as Experiment	Perceived as Promising
Complexity High	Perceived as Esoteric	Perceived as Valuable

The point of the first project is to make a splash, gain some experience, develop some processes, and brace yourself for what follows your success: the expectation that you can do it again—bigger, faster, and with much more complexity woven into the goals.

To pick a project, you must understand who your real customer is. This sounds easier than it is. The person or group asking for your help (and sometimes funding it) is not always the one who will use or benefit from your solution. Customer support can ask for help for a specific customer, or a manager for help with employee technical or leadership training, or an operations group for their internal constituency. You must know what the real problem is, and you get that only from the real customer.

Chapter 11: The Building Blocks

This can be an internal or an external customer. To pick a project, find yourself an unhappy customer with a business problem. These make for great e-learning projects because you're bound to make an impact if you focus on solving a customer problem. The more unhappy the customer or the bigger that customer's problem, the more room for success. However, remember the "ease of implementation" and "high business impact." High business impact doesn't mean you start with a core mission-critical area of the business; however, it can be exactly that if someone "picks" for you.

Then, pull out a calendar and circle a date for when you want to launch your pilot. Depending on how quickly you can assemble a team, pick a date that is 90 to 120 days out from your kickoff date. Plot backward from that date to today.

Next, engage your stakeholders. Stakeholders come in two flavors: supporters and naysayers—people who want to help see you succeed, and people who don't, respectively. Both types of stakeholders play an important role: one to encourage and support you, and the other to point out where you need to rethink, improve, or change what you're doing. The goal is to let both drive your requirements. The goal also is to turn your naysayers into supporters over time. That is one way you know you have succeeded.

Also make sure that your stakeholder team includes the customer or representatives from the customer community. An example of this is the VP of sales (your most important customer representative and stakeholder), including people on his staff who will have to use what you create. If the VP of sales has a training product or productivity problem you're solving, he might start off a bit upset. (Remember, he's the one with the business problem.) Focusing on his problem (more accurately, focusing on solving his problem) will help guide your project.

Partner with IT and drive to closure with as few stakeholders as possible, the first time. As success grows, stakeholders will become more supportive and more numerous. Avoid the naysayers in the "pilot." Don't waste time or energy on them until after you've landed and have results to discuss.

Conclusion

This chapter highlighted some of the key techniques that form the basis for an e-learning initiative within an organization. Without the tools described in this chapter, an e-learning initiative will face a difficult implementation. A review of the building blocks during the planning phases will help an organization avoid pitfalls during an e-learning implementation.

CHAPTER 12

ORGANIZING AN INTERNET LEARNING INITIATIVE

The Business Case for E-Learning

As previously discussed, the essential components of a successful e-learning model include e-communication, e-training, and e-assessment. The next question is, what are the steps that you can take to create success for your organization or ecosystem? This chapter discusses the eight steps required to organize an Internet learning program that generates productivity advantages:

1. Prepare a business justification for Internet learning in your organization.
2. Gather at least one senior executive's support and buy-in, including for the expected results, for a demonstration or pilot project.
3. Assess build versus buy options.
4. Implement the pilot.
5. Measure and report tangible results.
6. Plan the implementation based on the experience from the pilot project.
7. Involve stakeholders and create "owners."
8. Drive for results: Report progress frequently.

Hindsight Is 20/20: The Physics of Success

It does not matter whether your intentions with an e-learning initiative are to solve a departmental productivity problem, update your training and development function, or change or sustain a cultural change within your enterprise. Often, the most difficult thing is taking the first step.

It is fundamental to this section of the book and to your success and survival that you understand what we call the physics of success.

The first law:

It is easier to overcome momentum than inertia.

Simply put, it is easier to change direction if you are moving than if you are sitting still.

Get started.

The second law:

Small, attainable milestones create sustainable movement toward the bigger goal.

Simply put, a schedule with milestones no more than 10 to 15 days apart will rapidly and graphically illustrate progress.

Set your own target dates.

The third law:

Begin with supporters of the vision (zealots and evangelists).

Simply put, you can spend your time being successful, or you can spend your time trying to convince the naysayers that you will be successful if they ever get out of the way.

Ignore the buttheads.

The fourth law:

Speed and success creates gravity.

Simply put, the faster you achieve milestones, the more people and groups will want to participate in the successful implementation. Those additions to the team create critical mass, and eventually even the naysayers are drawn into the program. Resistance is futile. The gravitational pull of the program's success is too strong to choose another direction.

Go fast, be visible, and execute the plan.

Okay, this advice didn't actually include any physics; however, the relationships of the elements worked in a physics metaphor.

Prepare a Case for Internet Learning in Your Organization

This business justification establishes the value proposition for the organization to pursue Internet learning. When preparing a case for Internet learning, identify the synergy that is possible through all relevant components: e-communication, e-training, and e-assessment. If you have to focus on only one, begin with communications. Every organization needs more consistent and immediate communication results. For senior management, Internet learning is a mere tool that can influence the bottom line. Therefore, when creating a case, the emphasis should remain on organizational benefits rather than instructional details.

Often initial analysis begins with no more than some early "back-of-the-envelope" estimates that are eventually strengthened through results analysis. Such early analyses are useful in starting a business discussion. These discussions form the basis of brainstorming among managers and eventually assist in presenting alternative scenarios to various stakeholders. Because the process is still formative, no one has to feel too committed or attached to the proposal at this stage.

As part of preparing the case, sponsors should consider the following steps as part of organizing an e-learning initiative:

1. Base projections on needs analysis.

   Specifying the needs of customers (that is, the learner audience) is a critical first step to moving forward with the proposal. It also answers pressing questions of learners' willingness to adopt Internet learning. Are the needs knowledge based? Job or task based? Skills based? The answers impact the solution choices.

   Understanding demand for Internet learning is key to developing responsive programs and systems. Many Internet learning or web-based learning programs have failed because of overestimation of market demand or underestimation of the audience's potential requirements.

2. Identify potential savings.

   The next step may be a cost analysis. Vendors, associations, or consultants are often a useful source of cost information. Some of the most substantial savings in Internet learning are in travel, lodging, and time away from customers and clients. Cost savings appear more meaningful when the cost for scaling an instructor-led training program is compared with the cost of scaling an Internet-based learning program.

   At a global level, an Internet learning system might not only be adopted to reduce the cost of doing business for the training organizations, but also to reduce the entire organization's cost. Productivity advantages can be factored into the analysis. (See Figure 12-1.) For example, if an organization intends to increase the number of top-ranked performers by 10 percent through a more responsive Internet learning program, that difference could be factored into the organization's cost savings. If projects completed by trained and certified employees require 15 percent

Chapter 12: Organizing an Internet Learning Initiative

less time compared to others in sales support because of higher quality, the potential impact of additional trained and certified individuals on the bottom line for the project should be adjusted.

When extending into international markets, however, the cost of localizing content (translating into local languages) should be addressed. The incremental adoption of content among learners justifies the investment in localization. At Cisco, localization efforts are managed by respective theaters (regions) based on need within those markets for exams and courses.

The process aims at selecting and making available high-demand content in local languages. All content around a successful certification, exam, or course—including multiple-choice questions, simulation assessment items, course modules, practice tools, and presentation slides—are localized. Most content released in localized versions lags by a few months to what is released in English; however, the adoption among learners increases significantly when the localized content is released.

Figure 12-1   *Productivity Benefits of Internet Learning*

Productivity of Certified Staff

Q. Compared to noncertified staff, how productive are your staff?

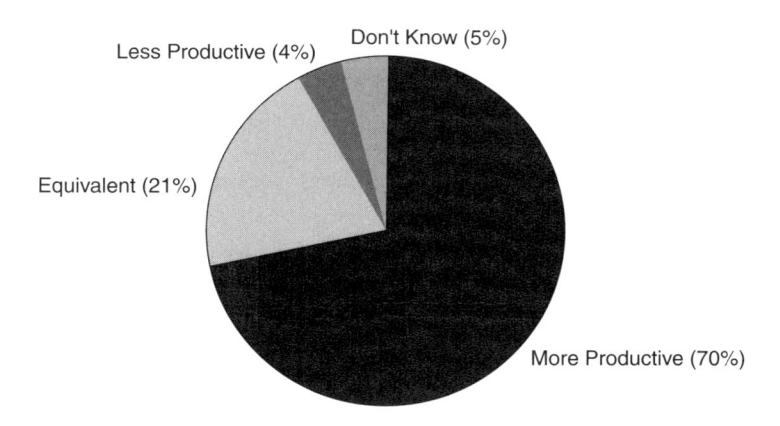

Less Productive (4%)
Don't Know (5%)
Equivalent (21%)
More Productive (70%)

Source: IDC's Certification Survey, May 2002   n = 100

3. Demonstrate reduced opportunity cost.

   Analyses that demonstrate quick contribution to the organizational bottom line are often the best means of bringing proposals to the attention of senior management. The savings make a compelling case for funding the project. (See Figure 12.1.) However, the savings cannot be demonstrated in the following year. From there on, it is a case of demonstrating compelling productivity advantages such as time to market, increased collaboration, increase in revenue, contribution to earnings, or improved morale to win the day for the prospects of e-learning.

4. Seek out revenue advantages.

   To succeed in identifying and expanding revenue streams, Internet learning planners could collaborate with the sales and marketing organization to understand the product development and distribution strategies. If learning is to assume a strategic dimension in the organization, learning planners must understand current and emerging trends in products, services, and skills. Training managers must meet other functional heads more than half way to demonstrate the willingness to develop and offer learning solutions that address the issues.

   If planners and decision makers can demonstrate a revenue advantage to the sales force as a result of anytime-anyplace access to skills-development tools, the case of Internet learning will become an even stronger consideration.

5. Contribute to the bottom line.

   The goal of working with sales may be to shorten the sales cycle, increase customer satisfaction, shorten "time to competence," or extend the general and specialized knowledge of the sales force.

6. Demonstrate benefits to customers.

   Customer satisfaction and customer loyalty generate repeat business. Planners can point to customer satisfaction advantages in a case for Internet learning if baseline data exists for comparison. If an organization's front-line employees (customer-facing teams) can

Chapter 12: Organizing an Internet Learning Initiative

maintain and improve customer relationships through better performance, the downstream impact of customer satisfaction and loyalty will be evident and measurable.

One way to enhance customer relationships is to establish a knowledge-sharing customer community through which discussion modules, information updates, product documentation, and even tips on troubleshooting are made available through a customer-centric portal.

7   Identify benefits to employers.

An astute employer may accrue numerous benefits by deploying Internet learning. Employers stand to gain the loyalty of employees who have greater and easier access to the tools of success offered by Internet learning. With a learner-centric program, an employee is more likely to view an employer as willing to invest in her growth and development—making the employer an attractive employment option for talented individuals.

8   Articulate benefits to the ecosystem.

In addition to employees and customers, resellers and vendors need to align closely with an organization to ensure that the weak links in a delivery chain are addressed. Benefits to an entire ecosystem translate to improved results for an organization. Using an e-learning system to improve the performance of partners and vendors and direct their focus on strategy evolution is an effective way to prove the value of learning.

9   Identify key dependencies.

A business case is not complete unless it highlights the relationships that the planners will form to ensure that the learning project succeeds. In terms of adoption, development, funding, and priorities, the training department responsible for instituting Internet learning works closely with other departments and business units. Identifying a set of stakeholders early ensures buy-in and support from across various teams later, during the adoption process. Leveraging other groups within the organization for the project facilitates the exchange of ideas, fosters collaboration, and helps identify content needs.

10. Propose a pilot.

    A short-term evaluation phase, also referred to as a beta or pilot effort, helps to define the project parameters. Because pilots are formative, planners maintain the option to redefine the project after the pilot implementation. However, having a project definition is a critical step in the business case development.

    For an Internet learning project, a pilot might include a series of voice, video, and text on demand or live-streaming presentations for the entire work force. It could include the introduction of existing video for viewing online, with accompanying exams available over the web. It might mean introducing some web-based courses to help employees realize the anytime-anyplace advantages of e-training. Whatever meets your needs, select a partial solution, implement it, measure the results, and report.

    A pilot effort keeps the skeptics at bay, manages expectations accordingly, and helps decision making within the group. The limited size, scope, risk exposure, and budget will allow individuals to understand that benefits will be evident without too much investment in upfront dollars. Pilot efforts offer a low-risk solution to a defined problem that most senior managers feel comfortable acting upon. The results on the effectiveness of the pilot eventually serve to determine the viability of the project in the long term.

Senior Management Sponsorship

Often, a valuable strategy during the senior management sponsorship phase is to demonstrate the link between learning and solving real problems—business problems. An executive sponsor who understands and sees the value can help build a strong case in the boardroom. His credibility can ride the project through skeptical questions and tight budgetary demands.

After an executive sponsor expresses willingness to champion the project, he should be well versed with the case and ideally offer input to the business case. The more an executive sponsor is involved in the pilot, the better he can represent the program to others.

Chapter 12: Organizing an Internet Learning Initiative

Hindsight Is 20/20: Cross-Functional Collaboration

Internet learning efforts occur several places around the organization. How are you going to align all these efforts—especially those that lie outside your charter?

Unless you are in an authoritarian company, it is almost impossible to get "all these efforts" in line. And the last job you want is to be the e-learning police department for the entire corporation.

If your CEO or some other executive said, "We're going to be completely moved to e-learning in 18 months" or something like that, you are probably experiencing the joy of multiple disjointed efforts. The executive always thinks that pronouncement gets the entire team on the same train as it leaves the station, headed toward the stated goal. More often, the reality is that without specific direction, everyone gets in separate rental cars and takes off in her own direction.

The way to be successful during a time of cross-organization experimentation and competition is to completely partner with the corporate IT and networking team. If you work with the IT team to address business problems, establish some standard tools that IT will endorse and support, and then demonstrate cost and learning effectiveness, you will succeed. The key is bringing the IT and the networking teams the business problem you are trying to solve early in the process, and getting their help to create the technical solution to that problem. The best part of this is that IT should extend their net police role to include e-learning tools and deployment, so you don't have to do it.

After these standards are clearly specified and accepted within the company, you get to encourage the experimentation and pilots that other groups want to do. The main thrust changes from compliance to convergence. Bringing in new tools, new processes, new disciplines, and new media is the only way to keep pace with the changing technology of the learning industry.

Doing that haphazardly and without discipline or process creates chaos for the learner community, and usually creates technical problems for IT. Learners cannot find all the content they need, even if it is out there; or if they find it, they don't have the right software or hardware to successfully launch it. Or the networking folks in IT find bandwidth impacts that negatively impact the company, or software that has surprise effects on other applications.

None of the preceding are desirable, and all are counterproductive to the goal of positively impacting the company and the business.

Assess Build Versus Buy Options

It doesn't matter whether the Internet learning pilot is built or bought; it is a pilot, not a long-term investment. Identifying economies of scale across large numbers of users might favor a build decision; however, the upfront cash outlay, uncertainty of success, and low estimates of adoption could sway others to pursue a more prudent "buy" approach. Your parameters will determine the right choice for each organization.

A combination scenario might include pursuing a buy decision in the early phases with an eventual migration to a build strategy after the project has a critical mass of users. Engaging with customized solution providers might be a strategy to launch the project and work through the learning curve. A six-month analysis with potential savings and adoption rates backed with a cost analysis might be the first step.

Hindsight Is 20/20: Picking Your Vendor

Suppose that 40 Internet learning vendors are waiting for you to call them back. I personally know the sister of the founder of one of them and recommend his company. How will you select the best partners from your list?

You will select your partner carefully if you are as smart as we think you are. Following are three key steps for selecting your Internet learning partner:

1. Establish and document business requirements for the projects, tools, and audiences. Do that with a cross-functional team representing IT, the audiences, and your project team.

2. Write the system and tool specifications with IT, and ensure that they do not contain proprietary information or requirements. Then, obtain cross-functional agreement on those specifications.

3. Put the specification requirements on a website where potential vendors, partners, and solicitors can access them, or in file, you can attach to an e-mail response to some vendor's inquiry.

If the vendor responds to your specifications in a way that indicates that their product matches your technical requirements, have someone check out its usability, performance, and alignment with your business and learning goals. Without the technical match first, you are both wasting your time. Don't forget to validate each vendor's financial viability.

Chapter 12: Organizing an Internet Learning Initiative

> The first time one of the vendors "incorrectly" fills out the specification survey, drop them like a hot rock; do this every time. It's a waste of time and sparse resources to work with a vendor that does not meet your technical requirements and does not accurately communicate that up front. "We can build an API," or "We will have that compatibility in three to four months," or variations on those themes are often the good intentions that pave a slow and winding road to delay or catastrophe.
>
> Exceptions to that rule are the few vendors that have an account and engineering team that is extremely compatible with your team. That is a rare and wonderful experience that often proves worth the hassle and the risk of waiting when you find it.

Implement the Pilot

A pilot test should aim to first assess learner interest in the program. Learner satisfaction with the tools, systems, applications, and content remains a critical consideration during any large-scale adoption. The pilot offers results that are specific to an organization. Financial data from the pilot is likely to form a more reliable basis for revenue, cost, adoption, and savings projections.

Because the data demonstrates what is attainable in the organization's context, management is also likely to rely on pilot results for funding decisions. Other management considerations that might emerge as a result of the pilot might include staffing questions, administrative policies, and customer service and support. Senior management can also review the effectiveness of the tools and technologies through the process. Some of the managers and executives might even participate as learners themselves to gauge the effectiveness of Internet learning.

Measure and Report Tangible Results

An evaluation of the impact of the pilot should be conducted to assess whether the effort met the expectations. If a gap exists in expectations and performance, that might cue planners into certain actions when moving forward with full-scale implementation.

If gathered through anecdotal data, although quantitative results are preferred, any data can make a compelling case for pursuing the full-scale adoption.

Prepare a Proposal for Expanding the Pilot

Relying on the data from the pilot, a planner can create an expansion plan that is unique and relevant to the organization's internal and external environment. The only nonintuitive part of this proposal is establishing a governance model (a structure or task force for managing the project).

Ongoing Governance

As the project unfolds, cross-functional collaboration is critical for success. Identifying the various team members representing the range of departments in a matrix organization allows broader perspective and alternative viewpoints on the project to be added.

Planners should identify and recruit a team of cross-functional participants to act as a small task force for the development and delivery of the program. The task force should be responsible for decision making on plans, priorities, and implementation. It should include the project manager, who would have the ultimate responsibility of ensuring project completion under time and budget. Having a governance model in place ensures that the stakeholders are not only involved at a macro level, but that they are also involved with the program's ongoing implementation.

Chapter 12: Organizing an Internet Learning Initiative

Hindsight Is 20/20: It Is a People Business

What types of people will it take to be successful—to survive this trip?

You need people who have developed software products: program and project managers who think differently and solve problems differently than the successful training professionals; not instead of, but in addition to those training professionals.

You need managers who think outside of their education box. You cannot solve new technology problems with older technology analysis. You need catalysts that cause, embrace, and successfully manage change. To be successful, you need account managers who can skillfully and artfully create and nurture the relationships you must form with other parts of the company or with outside vendors. You might need a poet or a few musicians to round it out so that you don't drift too far from the human values—interesting, engaging, and compelling; values that are often missing from content we all create. Not that you will actually be adding poetry or music (although you might), but these "creative types" may help keep your products "human" and as close to engaging or enjoyable as feasible.

Hire people who agree with your vision, values, and ethics, but who have a different perspective than you do. They openly and honestly question your direction and your tactics because they see different ways to accomplish the same goals. Usually, people make better decisions when they are forced to look at the problem and the solution from different, even opposite, angles. Constructive opposition makes the mind grow stronger and the thoughts clearer.

Separate from their skill sets, the e-learning team must be composed of flexible, creative people who know that during this experimentation they will experience the absence of success. You should add people to the mix who have a software development background and no training background at all. If there are any game programmers you can add, they will be helpful to the new pace and problem set your team will experience. Web folks and tools-integration people as well as video and audio specialists should be selected; again, these people probably have no training background. You still need all sorts of education and training professionals, product generalists, and people who are adventurous, action oriented, and driven to make a difference.

You also need some people who can sell and market your vision, programs, and products. Focus them internally at first because that is where you will experience the most resistance.

Finally, add business people to the mix. If you expect to have business impact, you need more business expertise and fewer hardcore training professionals in the management team. The decisions your team will be making are going to be more business- and less training-oriented. Business people does not translate into more finance people. This category includes business managers, marketing pros, sales managers, and IT professionals who want to build a new business and who hopefully have a passion for improving training programs.

Implement for Results

Preferably, whether created internally or outsourced to a learning solutions provider, Internet learning platforms or solutions should offer interoperability with existing systems, scalability for growth, open architecture for alignment, and plug-and-play capability for modular expansion. The platforms are discussed in more detail in the next chapter (Chapter 13, "Building an Internet Learning Solution").[1]

Relying on a standards-based platform should allow the system to work with several vendors. When deploying Internet learning, a proprietary solution could be an inhibiting factor if learners express an interest in a learning application that is not available from the vendor of choice.

Build to Scale

Irrespective of initial demand, an Internet learning program should be scalable (capable of expanding across regions and business units within an organization).[2] Internet learning may well become one of the most widely used applications within the organization and be accessed by every employee. Act global![3]

Chapter 12: Organizing an Internet Learning Initiative

Organizations with employees located worldwide should aim to offer content in local languages. For example, if a learner wants to search for content in Japanese, the available search tools should allow for that functionality. Similarly, the look and feel of the Internet learning platform should reflect the local language, colors, and designs to reflect regional needs.

Aim to Integrate

It is not only sufficient to have all the components of an Internet learning IT platform work cohesively, but it is also *essential* to have the platform aligned with legacy systems in other functional areas within the organization. An Internet learning solution will evolve in the context of existing systems—including human resources, finance, performance management, knowledge management, entitlements, and security—and the overall network infrastructure. Full integration means coordinating with the IT groups across functions for optimal deployment.[4]

Keep It Flexible

As an evolving productivity tool, Internet learning will continue to fuel demand for applications. Organizations will find it useful to integrate emerging publishing, authoring, and delivery applications with the Internet learning solution.[5]

Ensure Speed and Responsiveness

Organizations seldom have the luxury of lengthy development schedules. With Internet learning expected to deliver results in a short time frame, project managers must demonstrate speed in bringing a solution into production. With all the potential benefits of Internet learning, senior management will likely expect a fast turnaround on projects.[6]

Many technologies and tools are available in the marketplace, and a project planner is well advised not to be bound by a single technology. Being nimble and results driven in the organization might mean making multiple tools available from diverse vendors.

Conclusion

An integrated learning effort composed of e-communications, e-training, and e-assessment begins with a strong understanding of learner needs. Based on the needs, a business case with a projected cost-benefit analysis allows decision makers to proceed with a pilot project. With an understanding of the pilot's effectiveness, decision makers can take the next step of extending the e-learning effort.

Endnotes

[1] Crowley, Rick, "Blue Print for Enterprise E-Learning, A White Paper by Rick Crowley," Cisco Systems, Inc., June 2002.

[2] ibid

[3] ibid

[4] ibid

[5] ibid

[6] ibid

CHAPTER 13

BUILDING AN INTERNET LEARNING SOLUTION

The Business Case for E-Learning

> **NOTE** The chapter is based on a white paper, "Blueprint for Enterprise E-Learning," by Rick Crowley, Director of ILSG E-Learning Architecture.

Organizations have the option to build their own Internet learning architecture. In large-scale organizations or for application service providers, the economies of scale would justify such an investment into a solution and services architecture to meet the needs of internal and external learners. A comprehensive Internet learning solution architecture can be conceptually categorized into three groups: access tools, the learning applications, and the underlying network infrastructure. (See Figure 13-1.)

Figure 13-1 *Internet Learning Solutions Architecture*

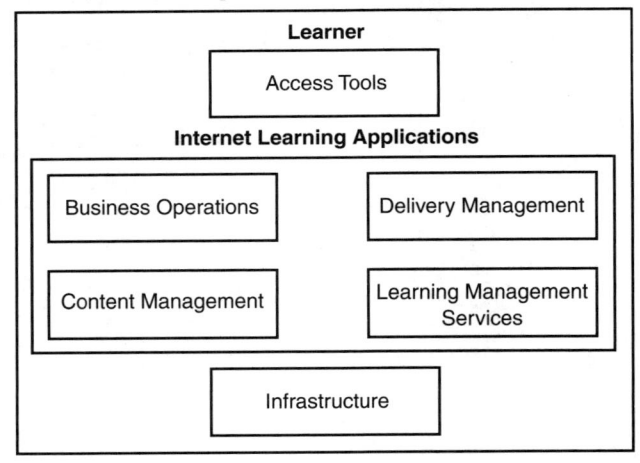

```
┌─────────────────────────────────────────────┐
│                  Learner                    │
│         ┌─────────────────────┐             │
│         │    Access Tools     │             │
│         └─────────────────────┘             │
│        Internet Learning Applications       │
│  ┌─────────────────┐  ┌─────────────────┐   │
│  │Business Operations│ │Delivery Management│ │
│  └─────────────────┘  └─────────────────┘   │
│  ┌─────────────────┐  ┌─────────────────┐   │
│  │Content Management│ │Learning Management│ │
│  │                 │  │     Services     │  │
│  └─────────────────┘  └─────────────────┘   │
│         ┌─────────────────────┐             │
│         │    Infrastructure   │             │
│         └─────────────────────┘             │
└─────────────────────────────────────────────┘
```

Access Tools

Access tools ensure anytime-anyplace access to the organization's learning resources. The access tools include synchronous (real-time) and asynchronous (on-demand) services for learner-friendly presentation of content. Essentially organized in a knowledge portal, access tools provide multiple audiences within an organization convenient access to courses, briefs, white papers, webcasts, videos on demand, and online tests. The internal or external audience may have a preference for a portal design that suits their needs based on their common interests.

Chapter 13: Building an Internet Learning Solution

Internet Learning Applications

Internet learning applications refer to components of an architecture. The applications provide the necessary tools for organizing, delivering, and managing content. The Internet learning applications fall into four broad categories:

- Business operations
- Content management
- Delivery management
- Learning management service (LMS)

Dividing the applications into four functional categories offers a framework for understanding their roles. The four functional areas map to the process of conception, development, delivery, and management. The areas also help to delineate roles and responsibilities and enable cross-functional collaboration. A flexible and scalable approach for e-learning allows best-of-breed functionality in each of the categories.

The following discussion offers a checklist of tools, systems, and applications to consider when deploying Internet learning. The discussion also outlines a host of tasks that should be the responsibility of learning managers within the organization's learning and development department. Depending on an organization's preferred business model, the following functions might be outsourced to or shared with other organizations.

Business Operations

Business operations include functions such as assessing needs, justifying costs, ascertaining the feasibility, evaluating results, and formulating instructional plans. From a systems, tools, and applications perspective, business operations should support the following services:

- **Learner experience**

    As part of business operations, the learning manager should define requirements for the user experience, such as use of downloads, video on demand, audio files, and simulation items and oversee the effectiveness of Internet learning solutions.

- **E-learning support**

  The E-learning support service should encompass all levels of support, including but not limited to learner support in the form of e-mail, an 800 call number, and online answers to frequently asked questions. The service should also provide support for all tools in the other administration and management areas.

- **Metrics**

  Metrics should be determined and tracked to evaluate satisfaction, penetration, usage, effectiveness, and relevance; the cost of training, tools, and processes; as well as their compliance with business objectives.

- **Online help**

  The online help service should be established to offer assistance for all Internet learning tools and services. It provides users and learners access to solutions for solving their problems themselves.

- **Security**

  The security function should ensure that access to applications and content relies on the users' and learners' roles. It also involves exam item integrity and confidentiality of learner performance records. In line with human resource policies within an organization, only supervisors should be allowed to view the employees' performance on online exams and assessments.

- **Business analysis**

  A cross-functional reporting tool offers the ability to provide reports on progress, usage, reusability of content, and overall business results for e-learning.

  A key of function of business operations is to provide decision input to assess viability and marketability of learning programs. Three critical functions must be addressed under business analytics: gap analysis, return on investment (ROI) analysis, and cost analysis.

  – *Gap analysis*

    The gap analysis function determines the difference between what learners need and want, as determined by job demands and performance evaluations, and their current knowledge based on assessment results. Data from the gap analysis will cue learning managers into which areas of content development are high priority and which programs are likely to be of most interest to learners.

– *Cost-benefit analysis*

A thorough cost-benefit analysis of a learning program is essential. Even though the learning program may not yield direct benefits for the learning department, its potential impact on the enterprise or its ecosystem should be documented for justification. Although many organizations launch successful Internet learning programs without much formal cost justification, an implicit cost-benefit in those cases might have institutively been evident to senior management.

– *Cost analysis*

The cost analysis function essentially addresses two processes: costing and cost-effectiveness. Costing deals with identifying and adding up the price of each component of a learning program so as to be aware of where and how much money was spent and where was it used. Over a period of time, it provides insights into cost-cutting and innovative changes in the process of how learning programs are created.

Cost-effectiveness of proposed programs, on the other hand, allows comparison of alternative options to help identify the one that might turn out as the most productive for an organization in the long run.

Hindsight Is 20/20: Dollars and Sense

Does Internet learning cost more to develop or deliver than classroom training?

Overall, it costs dramatically less to deliver e-learning, assuming that you are using existing networking capacity or incrementally adding capacity either via increased bandwidth or via edge technology (content-delivery networking) that stores high-bandwidth applications at the edge of your network. This enables you to optimize your current bandwidth capacity through more intelligent network usage.

Development cost comparison is not as simple or straightforward. A few years ago, media-based training cost three to five times as much as comparable classroom training. Today, the development cost is about 20 percent to 60 percent more for media-based content as compared to classroom training. However, dozens of new tools make it incredibly cheap to "snare and share" content across large numbers of people.

A lot of the training and communication between a product development group and their sales force can be accomplished by self-made videos that answer "the 10 most often asked customer questions" or "the 5 most interesting applications of this new technology." By using a video authoring tool (such as G-Force) that might cost less than $10,000 per desktop, the expert can create and deploy important content in small, useable chunks (also known as objects) to specific or generic audiences. This system pays for itself in less than one month by eliminating the many phone calls, e-mails, and interruptions the expert usually has to contend with during a normal day, not to mention renting studio and video crews to create more elaborate video messaging.

If video is not the best tool for your audience, how about creating audio and slides that are synchronized together? Whether a URL on a server or as a file you ship around or store in a published folder, there are now wonderfully easy, fast, and effective authoring tools that synchronize each slide with the appropriate voiceover. They can be edited separately, individually translated, or changed or reused, making this medium attractive.

Those are just two simple examples of how e-learning is faster, cheaper, and more easily created than classroom-oriented or written materials.

Content Management

Content management as a function should aim to make the development process convenient, consistent, and coherent for developers and learners. Content management involves enabling content providers to register, assemble, manage, and release learning content for delivery. One of the learning manager's key responsibilities should be to ensure that course authoring follows a common structure across the entire organization.

As course offerings increase in number, it is prudent to create content in three- to five-minute increments as reusable learning objects, including text, graphics,

Chapter 13: Building an Internet Learning Solution

assessment items, videos, and executable files. Creating content in small increments permits reuse and repurpose without having to re-create content. If repurposing and reuse is indeed an organization's goal, the authors of the content should follow guidelines to ensure that the learning objects are tagged and described accurately for other authors to take advantage of later. Use of structured learning authoring tools enables the author to assemble these learning objects into a course or lesson offering. In addition to making content available, content management also involves providing access to authoring tools and applications such as Macromedia Dreamweaver, Microsoft PowerPoint, or other tools.

Following are some of the content development tools, systems, and applications:

- **Workflow service**

    Workflow services ensure consistency of development across diverse authors. A workflow service helps to curtail any tendency on the part of authors to engage in scope creep—expanding the scope of the project over time.

- **Authoring tool**

    Authoring tool integration enables an author to incorporate past content, created elsewhere using a different tool, into new learning offering.

- **Registry service**

    Registry service ensures that the learning objects are tagged for later use and search by other authors. The learning objects are stored in a content storage system in a secure location for reuse and repurpose.

- **Object mining**

    Object mining services enable authors to locate learning objects that meet their search criteria.

- **Assembler services**

    Assembler services enable the author to drag and drop the desired learning objects from the object mining search result into a learning offering.

- **Content storage**

    Content storage services provide all the traditional library services for learning objects, including version control, notifications, history and reporting, and check-in/check-outs.

Content management enables managers to ensure that the development process is streamlined and the process remains efficient. By tracking the process and documenting best practices, learning managers can continually refine the process to meet the needs of the organization.

Delivery Management

When content is ready to publish, the delivery management function determines the best way to deliver it to users. Delivery management services include systems, tools, and applications used to support the following services:

- **Distribution management services**

    Business users should set up rules to help define how to manage content distribution. Through proximity management, the requested content is retrieved from the storage device that is closest to the learner. If the content is not retrieved immediately, it can be downloaded overnight for next-day availability.

- **Content presentation and request broker**

    When content is requested, dynamic delivery uses the learner's profile and preference to identify matching content. The request broker facilitates the transfer between internal and external applications and directs the learner to prepackaged content or to third-party vendor content, if needed.

- **Interaction results management**

    The delivery and distribution system tracks a learner activity while managing content delivery. The system reports those results back to learning management services (LMS) to track the history. The tracking is only temporary because all information pertaining to an individual is kept under the LMS.

The delivery management services make the promise of anytime-anyplace learning a reality for the learner. Through the distribution, presentation, and interaction results management, content becomes accessible to learners according to a predetermined service level.

Chapter 13: Building an Internet Learning Solution

Learning Management Services

LMS provides the user with the experience and the back-end systems to manage training transactions such as registration and validation. This is where learners access their e-learning environment and where their personalized tracking occurs. LMS manages all interactions here, including navigation, selection of learning offerings, and connection to delivery management services for delivery of learning offerings requested.

Following is a list of functions that LMS offers:

- **Personalization**

  The combination of a user's system profile and personal preferences provides the basis for personalizing the user experience and creating dynamically generated, personalized development plans. Profiles contain stored information about the learner, such as job title, organization, and location.

- **Search**

  By relying on a virtual repository at the back end, users can search or browse to find or add offerings. When a learner chooses to purchase an offering, the e-commerce capability within the LMS provides the payment functionality. When registration services receives notification of payment authorization, it notifies learner tracking services to add the offering to the learner's plan or marks the product for delivery.

- **Registration and tracking services**

  Registration enables learners to access offerings, register, and enroll in the offering from any portal location. A tracking feature tracks a learner's planned learning and progress through e-learning offering by recording the current status and history. Learners can modify their own learning plans, but they cannot modify learning plans proposed by their supervisors.

- **Assessment**

  Pre- and post-assessments are integrated with learning content to deliver a comprehensive curriculum that provides feedback to both learners and managers and adds value to the overall learning experience. Pre-assessments enable learners to study only the necessary material for a task at hand, thereby saving valuable time. Post-assessments provide results that are used to track completion status and are a key element for progress reporting.

- **Manager tools**

    Managers can access a learning plan or learning history for each of their direct reports. They can approve registration and add to their employees' future learning plans, and review employees' progress for both offerings and the related assessments. The manager tools can be tightly integrated with the corporate performance management system for greater effectiveness and accountability.

- **Evaluation**

    Evaluations enable LMS users to provide input for improved business operations or satisfaction with the tools, systems, and applications.

LMS serves as a means of management controls over the learning process. Availability, adoption, level of use, and performance of e-learning can best be assessed through an LMS system.

The Network Infrastructure

Based on the learning demand at the access level (both content volume and types of media), a robust network infrastructure is needed to meet the resulting bandwidth requirements. The network infrastructure ensures availability, scalability, security, quality of service, performance, and the ability to simultaneously deliver data, voice, and video. IP streaming and video-on-demand (VoD) applications are highly dependent on a high-capacity network. In many cases, the network infrastructure is the critical factor that determines the extent to which a learning manager may push the envelope for learning innovation.

Cisco Case Study: A Role for Content-Delivery Networks in Internet Learning

As Internet learning evolves to encompass more high-bandwidth applications and content, the role for content-delivery networks in the enterprise network infrastructure will increase. Organizations are more likely to use content-delivery networks (CDNs) for e-communication and e-training. A CDN is different from content management because it is a solution that is applied at the network infrastructure level.

A CDN ensures that learning content is available and accessible to any learner at anytime in a rich media format including voice, video, and data, no matter where in the world that learner might be located. The benefits of CDN are evident in the low-cost access to video, animation, and audio files. If an organization spends $5 for duplicating, packaging, and mailing a CD-ROM or videotape to 1000 sales employees every month for a year, for example, the organization could conceivably save approximately $60,000 per year by delivering content virtually.

A CDN offers the necessary infrastructure to cost-effectively bring learning and communications—live or on demand—to employees, partners, suppliers, and customers globally. The solution makes the learning process more engaging for learners and more cost-effective for the organization.

CDN offers the opportunity for developing a range of content choices for users at Cisco over a learning portal. As the Cisco sales force prepared for a changing marketplace in the first half of 2001, developers at Cisco created a learning environment that catered to diverse learners. (Some learners might prefer to listen to or watch an audio- or video-on-demand module, others may prefer reading a white paper or flipping through a PowerPoint slide.) The options made available through the delivery systems enabled learners to pick a learning modality of their own choice.

The Business Case for E-Learning

Challenge

Cisco needed to train a worldwide specialized sales team on a new solutions strategy, products, and implementation. The company initially considered flying all 300 members of the specialized sales team, training presenters, and coordinators to Orlando, Florida, for training. The total cost of this one-week training effort would have been significant. With a rental fee for the training venue, airfare to Orlando for attendees and presenters, and a week of hotel accommodations, food, auto rentals, and other expenses, Cisco estimated the total cost at about $750,000 or roughly $2500 per person.

Cisco, historically a frugal company, felt an even greater need to reduce expenses in a challenging economy. However, training the sales team without sacrificing the quality of the learning experience was still a priority. The company knew that using its own CDN solution to deliver more than 40 hours of interactive training could be done at a fraction of the cost of traditional training methods.

Solution

Using the Cisco CDN solution, Cisco delivered a live, four-day, training broadcast via Cisco Broadcast Servers in March 2001. In addition to serving the sales team, the training was also marketed to all sales organizations inside Cisco. An estimated 500 to 700 simultaneous IP streams were running per day, with a total viewing audience of nearly 2000 Cisco employees worldwide.

The Cisco Broadcast Servers streamed video programs to PC users over an enterprise network, enabling Cisco to deliver training directly to employee desktops. Between 10 and 30 sales specialists watched the live stream at each of the 16 regional offices throughout the United States and South America—without incurring a venue rental fee.

Subject matter experts presented the training via a live video feed broadcast from a TV studio at Cisco headquarters in San Jose, California. To deliver the content effectively, the Cisco Broadcast Servers encoded the analog streams to digital streams and used IP multicasting technology to distribute the content throughout the regions.

Chapter 13: Building an Internet Learning Solution

Desktop participants tuned into the programming using the Cisco IP/TV Viewer directly at their desktops or at a designated classroom training facility. When launching the viewer, participants chose the appropriate speed in which to watch the live video feed. They then watched the presenter, listened to the audio feed, viewed the presentation, and asked questions simultaneously.

The live event was recorded each day to capture the content for VoD playback at a later date, and to create a web-based training archive for Cisco employees.

Benefits and Results

The effort demonstrated the following outcomes and benefits for the program:

- **$600,000 cost savings**—The total cost of the 4-day, content networking training was approximately $108,000—a cost savings of more than $600,000 compared to the original estimate of $750,000 to train only 300 sales employees. Using IP/TV technology, Cisco actually trained nearly 2000 Cisco employees—a larger audience than originally intended. If Cisco had trained all 2000 employees using traditional methods at $2500 per person, the company would have spent roughly $5 million. Using its CDN solution, Cisco delivered this training to 2000 employees for less than $55 per employee.

- **High satisfaction ratings**—Although Cisco significantly reduced the training cost, the company did not sacrifice quality. By using high-quality bit rates and MPEG-1 media, Cisco generated high satisfaction ratings. Cisco surveyed participants of the training to measure training effectiveness, and preliminary results indicated that on a scale of 1 to 5, more than 70 percent of the attendees rated overall effectiveness between 4 and 5.

- **Wider audience reached**—In addition to saving Cisco training, travel, and lodging costs, the Cisco ECDN training provided reusable content to reach a wider audience.
- **Learning library built**—Any Cisco employee can download the 40 hours of reusable content—any time, anywhere—to receive training on the content around products and strategies.

The VoD was used for training new sales employees on how to deliver a product or solution pitch, and specific segments could be turned into sound bytes or video clips for use at Cisco seminars. The PowerPoint presentations and the VoDs were reused for channel and customer training. This reusable content also enabled Cisco employees who attended the training to review specific training segments and capture information they might have missed the first time.

Cisco captured all the participants' questions during the week and included this content in a searchable Q&A database, which was made available on the Cisco internal website. This Q&A database was an important resource for Cisco employees who were researching content networking products or strategies.

In addition to sales and marketing information, Cisco also delivered highly technical product information to systems engineers. One of the greatest benefits derived from delivering training using this method was the real-time, interactive, open forum for systems engineers and product management throughout the broadcast.

Using the Cisco IP/TV Question Manager, system engineers could click a question icon located on the IP/TV Viewer, type in a question, and click the Submit button. The presenters could then take the questions live and provide answers, making the training truly interactive for all participants. Not only did this provide product managers with direct customer feedback on technical product specifications and enhancements, but it also enabled product managers to solicit real-time feedback on future product road maps.

Chapter 13: Building an Internet Learning Solution

Collaborating to Create an Internet Solutions Architecture

Although the responsibilities for managing each of these asset groups at the previous three levels—access, applications, and network—may lie in different departments, incentives should be in place for those groups to collaborate for results. Strategic alignment will not only ensure efficient deployment at the outset, but it may also help create synergy across these assets. The three levels can effectively reduce the cost of maintaining learning tools, improve the entire organization's price-performance value proposition, and identify feature sets at each level that will yield productivity advantages for the organization.

Strong collaboration between the IT function, the learning function, and the production function under business leadership is essential for successful adoption. If the network infrastructure group is well tuned in to the learning needs, network managers can justify investment in higher bandwidth by consolidating similar demands from other departments. Communication across these functions can help the organizations reap significant benefits through creation of delivery of useful learning content by leveraging the existing and planned infrastructure investment.

To reduce its overhead in disparate competing platforms that coexist within an organization, business leaders should define standards tools and software platforms that an organization may be willing to support. Even though reporting of each of those departments may not lie under common business leadership, at minimum a dotted-line relationship across the distinct functions is necessary to ensure organizational success with Internet learning. Learning managers should be responsible for calling out the preferred tools and platforms based on learner needs and learner analysis. Executive support and incentives for an Internet learning initiative are critical to ensure that learning managers have the necessary voice in decisions that influence the requirements, standards, and functionality of an Internet learning solution.

Conclusion

An appreciation of the access, applications, and network layer of an e-learning architecture offers insights even in an outsourced learning situation. Learning managers should be cognizant that the e-learning architecture will form a useful component of the Internet learning process.

Metrics such as learner satisfaction, learner needs, and cost benefits can be gleaned from the reporting mechanisms within an e-learning architecture. Such insight is critical for the learning manager to understand the e-learning process within an organization. Managing the e-learning architecture is a commitment that can best be managed in collaboration with IT.

Remember, however, that having a robust mechanism for reporting helps to monitor demand, not generate it. Having an e-learning architecture provides a platform for e-learning delivery but does not generate demand for e-learning. High-quality, responsive content still rules the day when it comes to e-learning—and that must always top the list of priorities of a learning manager. In the pursuit of a sophisticated e-learning architecture, learning managers would be well advised to remember that a "build it and they will come" approach could add to the risk of failure.

CHAPTER 14

PRACTITIONERS' VIEWS ON THE BUSINESS ADVANTAGES OF E-LEARNING

Speaking with industry leaders, we captured their views on the business advantages that e-learning brings to an organization. They were asked whether e-learning is relevant for organizations in industries other than technology. The experts were asked to provide their insights on how organizations are addressing the integration of learning components and how organizations might adopt these components. In the interest of full disclosure, Cisco maintains business relationships with these Internet learning experts; however, they are known for their independent perspectives, which they were willing to share with us.

Convergys Learning Solutions: A Perspective on Deployment

Umberto Milletti, vice president of product and technology, Convergys Learning Solutions (formerly DigitalThink), is influential in the e-learning field. Convergys specializes in offering custom e-learning development and delivery solutions to corporate customers. In addition to cost savings, Convergys helps clients realize business transformation and value through e-learning deployment.

A relationship with Convergys Learning Solutions allows clients to reduce the need to invest in an internal infrastructure and applications platform. By partnering with Convergys Learning Solutions, clients can instead focus on driving business results through the dissemination of content across the enterprise. As a result, e-learning becomes a means of achieving organizational transformation, thereby increasing productivity.

Adopting Seamless Delivery Across the Enterprise

According to Milletti, the source of knowledge sharing, training, and assessment content in most organizations originates from a wide variety of sources. Some of the development takes place in-house; whereas training providers, partners, or suppliers undertake other development efforts. With the increased emphasis on just-in-time learning in most organizations, flexible content creation and distributed sources of content authoring has become the norm.

Chapter 14: Practitioners' Views on the Business Advantages of E-

Milletti advocates that organizations consider a platform of e-learning that seamlessly implements a single, consistent platform for content delivery for e-communication, e-training, and e-assessment that originates in various locations.

In addition to an integrated learning system, Milletti also advocates reusable tools to parsimoniously manage content. Content life cycle is a key consideration when creating knowledge sharing, training, and assessment items. Designing for reuse can extend the "shelf life" of content and reduce the cost of developing new curriculum. By creating content in modular chunks, organizations can salvage most of such content by repurposing it for use in a different business situation.

Achieving Productivity Gains Through an Integrated Approach to E-Learning

When asked what approach other organizations have assumed to harness the productivity advantages of e-learning within their environments, Milletti answered, "An approach of integration." For Milletti, combining e-communications, e-training, and e-assessment is as much an argument for assuming an integrated approach as it is for achieving productivity advantages.

Milletti cited Circuit City, a Convergys Learning Solutions customer, as a company that has assumed an integrated approach to develop e-communication, e-training, and e-assessment to generate productivity advantages. For Circuit City employees to effectively sell brand-name products, they must be able to access information about features and benefits at the right time. As a national retailer of household electronics and appliances, Circuit City uses a combination of communication, training, and assessment tools to ensure that its employees stay current on product details about brands offered at the store.

Circuit City deploys an e-communication tool for customized e-learning content for knowledge sharing with its employees to keep current on promotions, pricing, and product updates from manufacturers. The company fully utilizes e-training tools to offer store employees formal training toward their professional development. An employee's knowledge and training can then be assessed through one of Circuit City's certification exams. An employee's successful completion of such certification exams counts toward career advancement and promotion opportunities within the company.

Citing his own organization as an example of one that relies on an integrated approach to e-learning, Milletti explained how Convergys Learning Solutions supports its developer community. Based on a review of the marketplace, Convergys Learning Solutions identified a need to bolster the customer support and training activities with a certification program for developers using its L5 e-learning solution for Internet learning deployment. Convergys Learning Solutions L5 Developer—a certification—serves as a culminating component to the ongoing training, support, and hands-on guidance that Convergys Learning Solutions offers its L5 solution customers. The approach represents an example of combining assessment and training for optimal results within an ecosystem.

Viewing E-Learning as a Business Process Deployment

Milletti believes that organizations should view e-learning as business process improvement to achieve greater success with deployment. He thinks that for e-learning to be successful in an organization, senior management must be convinced of its benefits in a business context. When the business advantages become clear to senior managers, deployment often follows smoothly.

Milletti explains that the cost-benefit and business-value discussion is just as relevant to small and medium-size organizations as it is to enterprise organizations, and perhaps even more so. Small and medium-size organizations may view e-learning as part of their web services and rely on a partnership for best practices, content libraries, learning tools, and applications to support work-force development. According to Milletti, an external partnership for Internet learning deployment makes even more business sense when organizations are faced with budgetary constraints.

ElementK: A Question of Leadership

Bob Mosher, executive director at ElementK, is recognized as an e-learning thought leader. Conversations with him provided a perspective that presents a simple, yet profound, recommendation to people who are thinking about adopting e-learning for business in their organizations. Mosher believes that the extent of commitment to Internet learning on the part of managers is a function of their commitment to productivity and their belief that learning can help generate the desired productivity.

According to Mosher, if line managers view Internet learning as an opportunity to "buy back time" and keep employees at work for 40 more hours each year, the advantage is lost. The opportunity to integrate learning into the business process is where the productivity returns should be sought—not in the mere saving of time.

Based on his experience of working for a multitude of organizations, Mosher believes that knowledge sharing is a "sleeping giant" in terms of its potential to impact organizations' learning processes. Communication tools such as e-mail, real-time chat, electronic meetings, FAQ sites, and learning portals present a cost-effective way to improve the work environment and productivity. According to Mosher, knowledge sharing will continue to offer a user-friendly segue into making learning permeable throughout the organization. Workers are likely to be less resistant to knowledge-sharing tools because of their community-driven approach.

With respect to e-training, Mosher maintains that organizations should seek to empower workers so that they can make smarter decisions for their organizations. E-training is a tool that improves the decision-making environment throughout the organization. According to Mosher, it is through learning and empowerment that knowledge workers will emerge from the ranks of the work force.

According to Mosher, assessment tools such as certification exams, online tests, and quizzes have been the missing link in many organizations. Assessment is about accountability. Being able to demonstrate results through learning requires steps such as online exams, quizzes, task analysis, competency mapping, and skills-gap analysis. In organizations where even job descriptions are not mapped out, however, the notion of having individuals conduct thorough pre- and post-assessment might be a steep task.

Basically, organizations must consider the existing attitude toward learning within their organization. If training is still being viewed as an activity-driven event with little or no relevance to organizational bottom line, line managers will not embrace the e-learning efforts. For Internet learning to make any headway, the line managers must buy into the notion that offering learning opportunities offers productivity improvement. If line managers never perceived training as an agent for boosting productivity, the chances of them perceiving Internet learning as a productivity tool will also remain slim.

"Adopting Internet learning might not be as simple as turning on a light switch; it won't just happen because content is available on a server somewhere," says Mosher. "Purchasing IDs is not the answer." Decision makers should invest in their culture to integrate learning into the business as an inherent process rather than as an event-driven activity. Beginning with knowledge sharing, applications might have more chance of adoption because the value of knowledge sharing is more evident and intuitive to line managers.

Organizations can move forward by adding on to tutorial, virtual labs, and blended learning solutions that combine Internet learning with existing face-to-face classroom instruction. According to Mosher, organizations starting from their present place and moving forward from there will more likely bring about organizational change. With Internet learning, Mosher postulates, the classroom might be the best place to begin deploying it.

The transition to an environment that is highly independent and learner driven could conceivably create resistance within an organization; however, much like the migration from a mainframe to client environment, Mosher believes that information technology's transition to Internet learning is inevitable; however, he warns not to expect changes at light speed. "Although there will always be revolutionary approaches in education, they will only be adopted at an evolutionary rate," says Mosher, reading from a quote hanging on his office wall. He believes that productivity results in the long run, and that it is a function of organizational culture responding to Internet learning as much as it is a function of technology.

Cisco Communities: Building Customer Loyalty

It might seem strange at first to think about e-learning assisting with market positioning and branding, but to Don Field, senior manager, at the Internet Learning Solutions Group of Cisco Systems, applying e-learning to strengthen brand loyalty by creating favorable customer experiences is not a new concept. We discussed with Field his experiences with the Cisco Certifications Community were discussed, a project dedicated to knowledge sharing globally among Cisco-certified engineers as a free benefit to being certified.

Here's how he describes it: "If your market segment is broadband ready, then your brand is ready for a customer loyalty program or an affinity program that is built around web-based exchange of knowledge and information." You have seen at least one financial services organization create an exclusive e-community for its clients that offers financial tools, retirement calculators, access to online financial mentors, tax tips, and links to selected articles as a useful way to build trust and loyalty among customers.

Building brands is about creating positive, meaningful experiences. Advertising, public relations, storefronts, logos, and packaging are one-way interactions that contribute to building the expectation of an experience. Customer service is a two-way interaction (a direct experience), but the challenge is controlling the cost and quality of such interaction. Utilizing e-learning tools can enable organizations to better manage the customer experience on a one-to-one basis while also proactively managing the cost and inconsistency of each interaction. The goal is to share knowledge for positive customer experiences that result in increased loyalty to the brand, and eventually increased revenue.

Based on his experience with customer communities, Field states that creating a bundle of knowledge-sharing services through a program over the web for current customers can have several benefits:

- Strengthens brand franchise
- Rewards loyalty of customers, resellers, and partners
- Lowers program management costs
- Scales as needed at minimal incremental cost
- Integrates with existing customer-relationship tools

So how does a brand manager think through building this kind of a community using e-learning tools?

Knowledge Sharing Through Communities

According to Field, customer communities have existed in the form of bulletin boards, message boards, forums, and "communities of interest" for a while. Getting customers to share their brand experience is a common practice on many websites. With tools for e-learning, organizations can share alternative product uses, beta products, troubleshooting tips, and testimonials with and among customers to seed such discussions. Besides branding, the forums can become a useful tool for gauging customer satisfaction and customer needs for current and future brand attributes. The success of a community is related to the openness encouraged there and a focus on shared-learning rather than marketing. It is an interesting phenomenon that the absence of overt marketing content increases the actual marketing value and impact of these kinds of forums or communities.

Knowledge Sharing Through Engaging Content

The experience at Cisco has demonstrated that a game based on creative content and testing from something as simple as the product manual can engage customers in a more successful way than the manual itself. Because of that interest, they are more likely to retain the knowledge or skills that might lead to reduced support calls and improved customer satisfaction ratings. If the brand experience is positive, not only is repeat purchase more likely, but also the purchase of complementary products is likely enhanced. Most customers want to understand the products and services they buy, at least enough to use them independently. Offer that opportunity, and their surprise will increase their satisfaction with the product and the company.

Knowledge Sharing Through Events

Cisco has actively engaged in the use of video or audio over the web to create live broadcast events where customers participate via call-ins, live demonstrations, product-launch events, technical seminars, or training. The opinion leaders from among the customers value exclusive events where they might feel part of a select group. Having advocates of the brand within the customer base can pay off in brand-building many times over than mere advertising. *Exclusive* might mean earlier access to the event than others, or it may mean "only" certain people are invited. Either way, they are special events for special customers, who appreciate that kind of relationship.

Justifying the Investment

Essentially, the value on investment for such a program will be assessed by measuring the increase in customer satisfaction and loyalty toward the brand. Evaluation of a limited affinity program implemented for a thousand or so customers can demonstrate an increase in satisfaction or loyalty metrics within a six- to nine-month period. Knowing the quantitative impact on customer loyalty would offer planners a clear sense of cost benefits. The amount of success will shape the future investment in these kinds of programs. The ease of scaling up a successful program makes small-scale piloting a safe and financially sound action. These kinds of tactical programs will shape a strategic change in a company's customer service policies when they are well done, have an impact, and are measured accurately.

Conclusion

The knowledge-sharing and business-optimization benefits of e-learning have the potential to permeate throughout an organization, its partners, and their customers. In an age of evolving electronic media, taking advantage of e-learning tools for customer loyalty, improved productivity, and innovative processes will require abandoning a stove-piped approach in favor of collaboration across functional lines. You may start, pilot, or experiment in a variety of silos, but the organization is best served by the convergence of the silos. Collaboration will eventually lead to stranger bedfellows within your organization than training and marketing working together for a competitive advantage.

That will be an odd circumstance, but an incredibly good outcome, demonstrating strategic focus on the organization's productivity, brand, and success of the entire organization. This also harnesses all the company's best intentions on a unified, clearly delineated set of programs and tactics instead of each organization trying to serve their narrow version of the mission. Who would have thought that learning could bring them together?

EPILOGUE

Where Do We Go from Here?

As Cisco went through these seven years of experimentation and a variety of implementations, results, and reporting, it became obvious that organizational impact needed to be broader than any one group or department could create. The individual group successes were a definite sign that larger, integrated successes were possible.

So, John Chambers suggested an initiative called Cisco University be undertaken to assure that this company developed its employees in better, more creative, and more effective ways. He asked that Cisco University (CU) become the place where "employees train for excellence in their current job, but develop and prepare for jobs they will have in the future."

That means that CU would need to offer learning opportunities beyond traditional training, and beyond the common e-learning offerings.

Because Mr. Chambers is the CEO of Cisco Systems, the initiative known as CU was created, funded, and launched in spring of 2004.

CU is formulated around the concepts of Education, Exposure, and Experience. It will ensure that people have or develop the skills and knowledge to perform their current job in an exemplary manner, exposure within Cisco's broad leadership community to see or be offered other career opportunities, and experiences that prepare employees for broad, long-lasting success in their career at Cisco.

We are building this capability because of the strategic importance of people to this and any company or institution. Cisco is using E and other learning/teaching media because of the incredible success of the network deployed content: quick, efficient, and consistently to large, dispersed audiences.

The strategic impact of e-learning demonstrated in the business cases sited in this book (and so many more cases that could not be included) support all the early adopters and experimenters in e-learning. The continued improvement in the tools that enable us to share knowledge, teach skills, and then test and validate our confidence in the competence of employees are clear evidence that e-learning will become a larger and larger part of the public and private sector's education/training/learning implementations.

However, e-learning will never eliminate the need for people who are skilled in teaching and communicating. That is not the point, or the intent.

E-based learning simply shifts the priority in the learning process from the instructor's availability to the learner's control. The learner decides how and when to engage an instructor, a mentor, or a coach, and when to learn from a book, a video, a simulation, or a game. The learner decides when during the day or night, and where to employ those wide range of choices. The learner chooses which way works best at that moment and at which location.

That control and flexibility allows us to learn when we are most motivated and most interested. It allows more control of our present schedules, our future, our career, and our lives. And it allows companies and institutions to make learning a part of their strategic advantage in the marketplace, a key retention tool, and a tactical solution to the need to develop talent within the ranks of their employees.

E-learning works, and the successes of the past seven years (only partially documented here) will drive greater experimentation, more creativity, and even more human and business success over the next seven years.

Combining the Internet and education eliminates the barriers that stand between people wanting a different life and the future they dream about.

Combining the passions of employees and the goals of a company increases the success both experience.

INDEX

A

access tools, 158
accountability, increasing within training industry, 35
analyzing skill gaps, 135
applications, components of Internet learning solution architectures, 159
    business operations, 159–161
    content management, 162–164
    delivery management, 164
    learning management services, 165–166
assembler services, 163
assessing
    CCIE certification program
        benefits to candidates, 50
        benefits to employers, 49
    Cisco Networking Academy students, 81
    Internet learning programs, build versus buy options, 150–151
    learning needs, skill gap analysis, 135
assessment tools, 48

B

BearingPoint approach to e-learning engagement, 137

benefits
    of certification to employers, 110–111
    of Cisco Networking Academy Program to Cisco Systems, 83–84
broadcast video over IP, 39
build versus buy options, assessing for Internet learning programs, 150–151
building extended enterprises, 105–106

C

"Can the Internet Help Solve America's Education Problems?", Lessons from the Cisco Networking Academies" study, 82
case studies, Internet learning solutions
    content-delivery networks, 167–169
    management collaboration, 171
CCIE certification program, 48
    benefits to candidates, 50
    benefits to employers, 49

CDNs, case study, 167–169
certification programs
    benefits to employers, 110–111
    CCIE, 48–50
        benefits to candidates, 50
        benefits to employers, 49
    Cisco Partner Program certification, 119–120
    launching, 122–123
        development phase, 123–130
    neutral, 118
    sponsoring, 118
change management, e-learning as function of, 137
channel partners, 96
    Cisco Partner Specialization program, 97
    feedback concerning PEC, 101–102
    learning challenges of, 98
choosing e-learning projects, 137–139
Cisco IP/TV Question Manager, 170
Cisco Networking Academies Program, LDC initiative, 85–86
Cisco Networking Academy Program, 78
    assessment tasks, 81
    background, 79
    benefits to Cisco Systems, 83–84
    curriculum, 80
    impact of, 82
    in underserved communities, 82
    learning components, 80
    train-the-trainer model, 80
Cisco Partner Program certification, 119–120
Cisco Partner Specialization program, 97
collaboration of Internet learning program managers, 171
content development, 44–47
content life cycle management, 134
content storage services, 163
content-centric e-training, 42

cost savings
    from Internet learning, 97
    of e-learning programs, reseller survey findings, 52–54
    to partners from PEC, 103–105
cost-benefit analysis of learning programs, 161
creating certification programs, 122–123
    development phase, 123–130
credibility, increasing within training industry, 35
cross-functional collaboration of Internet learning programs, 152–154
cross-functional management of learning components, 133–134
Crowley, Rick, 158
curriculum, Cisco Networking Academy Program, 80

D

delivery management, 164
deploying
    e-communication, 37
    learning tools, 134
    productivity cycle, 73–76
developing certification programs, 125
    business analysis, 123–124
    program development, 125–126
    program implementation, 127
    program management, 128–130
distributed authoring, 135

E

e-assessment, 48
    CCIE certification program
        benefits to candidates, 50
        benefits to employers, 49

e-communication
    as productivity tool, 36–37
    fostering retention and motivation, 37–38
    VoIP, 39–40

Equant merger with Sita
    benefits to Equant, 114
    legacy network integration, 112–113
    reliance on certified engineers, 113

e-training
    content development, 44–47
    development model, 44
    evolution of, 41–43

evolution of e-training
    at Cisco, 41–43
    content development, 44–47

expanding Internet learning pilot program, 152

extended enterprises, 96
    building, 105–106

F-G-H

FELC (Field E-Learning Connection), 98
flexibility of Internet learning programs, 155
functional integration of learning components, 133

I

impact of Cisco Networking Academy Program, 82
implementing pilot for Internet learning programs, 151
    expanding, 152
    measuring results, 152
increasing accountability within training industry, 35
initiating e-learning projects, 137–139

integrating
    learning components
        cross-functional management, 133–134
        deploying tools, 134
        functional integration, 133
        knowledge-sharing tools, 132–133
    Sita and Equant legacy networks, 112–113
        benefits to Equant, 114
        reliance on certified engineers, 113

Internet learning programs
    aligning platform with legacy systems, 155
    build versus buy options, assessing, 150–151
    cross-functional collaboration, 152–154
    flexibility of, 155
    organizing, 142
    pilot
        expanding, 152
        implementing, 151
        measuring results of, 152
    preparing a case for, 143–148
    scalability of, 154
    senior management sponsorship, 148–149

Internet learning solution architectures
    access tools, 158
    CDNs, case study, 167–169
    learning applications, 159
        business operations, 159–161
        content management, 162–164
        delivery management, 164
        learning management services, 165–166
    management collaboration, 171
    network infrastructure, 166

ISO 9001 recertification training program, 41

J-K

Johanson, Per, 113
just-in-time learning, 71–73

knowledge sharing, 132–133
    as productivity tool, 36–37
    fostering retention and motivation, 37–38
    VoIP, 39–40
Kramer, Mark, 83

L

launching certification programs, 122–123
    development phase, 123–130
LDC (Least Developed Countries) initiative, Cisco Networking Academies Program, 85–86
learner buy-in, 136
learner-centric training, 43
learning applications, 159
    business operations, 159–161
    content management, 162–164
    delivery management, 164
    learning management services, 165–166
learning components of Cisco Networking Academy Program, 80
learning management services, 165–166
learning manager, role of, 159
legacy systems, interoperability with Internet learning programs, 155
line functions, 71

M

managing content life cycle, 134
measuring results of Internet learning pilot program, 152
module centric e-training, 42
Murnane, Richard, 82
Murora, Beth, 84

N-O

network infrastructure of Internet learning solutions, 166
neutral certifications, 118

object mining, 163
organizing
    Internet learning programs, 142
    physics of success, 142
    preparing case for, 143–148
    Internet learning projects, localization, 145

P

partner certification, Cisco Partner Program certification, 119–120
PEC (Partner E-Learning Connection), 97–99
    cost savings to partners, 103–105
    features of, 100–101
    feedback from partners, 101–102
    financial benefits of, 51
performance centric e-training, 42
physics of success, 142
pilot tests for Internet learning programs, 148
    expanding, 152
    implementing, 151
    measuring results, 152
portal centric e-training, 42

portals, 134
   PEC, 99
      cost savings to partners, 103–105
      features of, 100–101
      feedback from partners, 101–102
Porter, Michael, 83
preparing case for Internet learning, 143–148
   pilot programs, 148
productivity
   impact of certification on, 110
   increasing through e-communication, 36–37
      fostering retention and motivation, 37–38
      VoIP, 39–40
   through certification, 49
productivity cycle, deploying, 73–76

Q-R

quadrant charts, selecting e-learning projects, 138–139

registry services, 163
resellers
   channel partners, 96
      Cisco Partner Specialization program, 97
      learning challenges of, 98
   Cisco Partner Program certification, 119–120
   feedback concerning PEC, 101–102
   Walker Information survey findings, 52–54
retention, enhancing through e-communication tools, 37–38

S

scalability of Internet learning programs, 154
selecting e-learning projects, 137–139
senior management sponsorship of Internet learning programs, 148–149
Sita merger with Equant
   benefits to Equant, 114
   legacy network integration, 112–113
   reliance on certified engineers, 113
skill gap analysis, 135
SMEs
   demand for, 34
   distributed authoring, 135
sponsoring certification programs, 118
stakeholders, role in launching e-learning projects, 139
starting e-learning projects, 137–139
student assessment, Cisco Networking Academy Program, 81

T

tools, deploying, 134
Toyota productivity cycle, deploying, 73–76
training programs, Cisco ECDN solution, 169
train-the-trainer model, 80
Tymer, Ellie, 71

U-V

underserved segment of Cisco
   Networking Academy Program, 82

VoD (video on demand), 40
VoIP as e-communication tool, 39–40

W-X-Y-Z

Ward, George, 78
workflow services, 163